Through the Storm

Through the Storm

Dr. Cassundra White-Elliott

Through the Storm is a work of non-fiction. All scripture are from the King James Version of the Holy Bible.

The stories included in the sections of each chapter titled *Glimmers of Hope* are excerpts written by anonymous people, unless otherwise noted.

Published by CLF Publishing, Inc.

Cover by Senir Design. Contact information: sd_grpx01@yahoo.com

Printed in the United States of America.

Dedications

For Handsome

Thanks for all your love and support.

For my brothers:

Noah, Rod, and Aug

Table of Contents

Introduction

"Many are the afflictions of the righteous: but the LORD delivereth him out of them all" (Psalm 34:19). In this life, the inhabitants of planet earth, who are the elect of Christ, the children of the Most High god, Jehovah, will be afflicted with trials, tests, and seemingly unbearable circumstances. But, the Lord, our God, will surely deliver us from them all. With this notification of afflictions that is taken directly from the word of God, there is no need for us to be shocked or dismayed by the fiery darts that are sent by the enemy or by the circumstances that God allows us to go through. Instead, we should expect them. With our expectations of afflictions and in an effort to navigate through them without a blemish or stain, we need to learn how to put our trust in the Lord for instructions on putting the fires out so that we can carry on with our lives. Remember, tests, obstacles, insults and injury come to build us as we go through our faith walk, so that we may minister to someone else.

Christ came to set the captives free and to give us life and life more abundantly (John 10:10b). I come to encourage all of my fellow brethren to keep your heads uplifted and your spirits renewed, even in the midst of the storms of life. Keep your heads lifted toward the hills from whence cometh our help. Remember, our help comes from the Lord (Psalms 121:1-2).

Initially when pondering the subject matter that would be contained within the pages of this book, I thought to possibly give it the title *In the Midst of the Storm* because of all the storms that encapsulate us during our lifetimes. After tossing the title around in my head, I considered its implications. To me, *In the Midst of the Storm* is very indicative of periods that we have in our lives. However, *In the Midst of the Storm* seems to have a negative connotation as well. Very subtly, it implies that a person is in a storm and that he/she has been placed there permanently. Conversely, I found the title **Through the Storm** to be more appropriate because its connotation is two fold. On one hand, the title implies that a person has been in a storm and on the other hand, he/she has successfully navigated through. **Through the Storm**, as opposed to *In the Midst of the Storm*, breeds hope.

Through the Storm is a source of inspiration for those who have ever experienced a storm in life, those who are currently experiencing a storm and those who will soon enter into a storm. This book will cover the storms of depression, education, finances, self concepts, losses, death, and broken relationships.

Let us engage in a word of prayer before you commence your reading.

Heavenly Father,

We exalt your name as we come before you thanking you for this day. We thank you for breathing the breath of life into us once again. We come into your courts with thanksgiving because you are so gracious, so loving and so kind. You have seen us through the tough times when we did not think we were going to make it. You have seen us through the perilous storms that sought to devour us. You gave us strength and you carried us when we were too weak to make it on our own. Father God, we thank you for all that you have done. We are not worthy of your goodness, your mercy or your grace, but because of who you are- you saw fit to continue to bless us. After you hung on the cross at Calvary for our sins, we should not dare to ask for another thing. But we continue to cry out and ask anyway. And you continue to come to our rescue. Our Father, which art in Heaven, where would we be without you? It is because of you that we are here. Oh, how we thank you Lord. Oh, how we praise you, oh Lord of Lords. Thank you for being our rock. Thank you for being our way maker, our peacemaker, our joy, our strength, our all-in-all. Father, we thank you for your divine protection and the cloak of precious blood that shields us from all hurt, harm, and danger. We thank you for lifting the scales from our eyes so that we may see clearly and for opening our ears so that we may hear what thus saith the Lord. Father, as we read this book, let your words pierce our hearts as we meditate on them. Father, help us through the storms that we encounter in this life and see us safely through, in Jesus' name.

Amen.

At the end of each chapter is a section titled *Glimmers of Hope*. This section includes short stories by other writers (most of whom are anonymous) to help enrich the various topics discussed in the particular chapter. Read these stories and let the Holy Spirit continue to minister to you.

One

The Cloud of Depression

Through the Storm was duly inspired by the avaricious cloud of depression that decided to hover overhead of my daily existence in the latter part of 2007. Although I found it extremely difficult, I was once again compelled to not be defeated by just another snare that the enemy, the trickster, set for me. Once again, or more appropriately I should say *continuously*, he has exerted pernicious efforts to snatch the very life out of me by causing me to wallow in despair and to believe that I had been overcome by failure when in actuality and all reality, I was just experiencing a temporary set back. During those cloudy days, I had to remind myself daily that even though I was a target of the enemy, I am and will always be a child of the Most High god, Jehovah, who is my rock, my stability.

In my last book ***Dare to Succeed by Breaking through Barriers***, I discuss many barriers people find themselves faced with and the keys to successfully breaking through and overcoming those barriers.

However, upon the release of the book, I too found myself faced with barriers, barriers in their multiplicitous form. Just as I reminded my readers, I had to continuously remind myself that one of the benefits of being God's child is the ability to be victorious in all battles, which comes from standing firm and continuing to fight the good fight of faith believing that I am an over comer and a conqueror as told to me in Romans 8:37.

During the midst of these seemingly perilous times, a dear friend gave me a cd by the Williams Brothers. While driving and listening, tears streamed from my eyes as I listened to the words of one particular song, "Still Here." The song says,

Heartaches, I've had my shares of heartaches, but I'm still here
Trouble, I've seen my share of troubles, but I'm still here
Bruises, I've taken my lumps & bruises, I but I'm still here
Loneliness, I've had my share of loneliness, but I'm still here

Through it all I've made it through another day's journey, God kept me here
I've made it through another day's journey, God kept me here
Lied on, many times I've been lied on, but I'm still here
Burdens, I had to bare so many burdens, but I'm still here
Dark days, I've had my share of dark days, but I'm still here
Disappointments, I've had so many disappointments, but I'm still here

Chorus
It's by the grace of God, that I'm still here today
He was always there, no matter what came my way
I felt the presence of him, in my time of need
Standing right there, just to seal my faith

Chorus
I made it (I made it)
I made it (yes, I made it)

I'm still here (I'm still here)
A lot of folks say that I wouldn't be here tonight, but I made it (I made it)
By the grace of God , yall (yes, I made it)
I'm still here (I'm still here)

I have to lay awake in the midnight hour sometimes, tossing & turning (I made it)
All night long (yes, I made)
Have anyone had to lay awake all night long sometime (I'm still here)
Tears in your eyes wandering what the next day was gonna bring (I made it)
God kept has arms around you, yes he did (yes, I made it)
You made through the trails (I'm still here)

Come on let me see those hands in the air
I made it, I made it (I made it)
I made it, I made it (yes, I made it)
I made it, I made it (I'm still here)
Through it all (through it all I'm still hereeee)

To me, every word uttered in this song exemplified both my past and present experiences. But the triumph in it all was the victory that was in my grasp. I knew that I had to praise my way through to a new season.

But before victory was attained, with all the burdens that weighed heavily upon me, day after day I seemed to sink further and further, deeper and deeper into an abyss of depression. I fervently tried to shake it. But to avoid the daily pressures, that my life was consumed with, I would sleep later and later each day, in an attempt to avoid the world at large, which seemed to want to swallow me whole. This continued to the point where I would even turn the phone off to avoid not only the insolent bill collectors but also loved ones. I didn't avoid loved ones because I didn't love them any longer. No, I avoided them because I did not want them to hear in my voice the anguish I was enduring.

The irony of it all, though, was that I believed the word of God, and I knew unequivocally that He had not forgotten me and that he would not forsake me, for He had given me a life of blessings and he had already shown me glimpses of a very bright and promising future. He had given me two new teaching assignments (on top of the others that I had), my books were doing well and selling all over the country, my children and I were healthy, we had food to eat and a roof over our heads, but I was caught up in emotional and financial troubles that did not seem to want to dissipate any time in the near future.

Despite my inner beliefs, I walked around in a fog. I didn't even feel like myself, the achiever, the risk taker, the encourager of others, the friend, or the mother. I felt as though I had nothing to offer, to anyone, not even to myself. Then, as a result of trying to sort through things and make the best plan possible with what God afforded me on a daily basis, I began to suffer from excruciating headaches. Night after night, I went to bed with headaches that prevented me from thinking, even about the slightest of topics. I still wanted to escape all reality. I wanted to wake up to a new day that was filled with brightness and hope, not gloom and despair. That, however, was not in my immediate future. I felt like the devil was trying to steal my mind, but I was not about to relinquish it to him- no matter what.

In addition to the headaches, I suffered a loss of appetite. This in and of itself is not surprising because most people who suffer from depression and/or stress either overeat or under eat. For me, when I am dealing with a lot of stress, I tend to under eat. Food is always the last thing on my mind. This time, however, I didn't even remember to eat, let alone think about it. I would look around and more than half the day would be gone, and I would not have eaten a thing. It wasn't until someone actually told me to eat that I gave it a thought. Even to me, this sounds surreal. But, it happened.

Finally, when I began my new teaching assignment, the headaches and the loss of appetite decreased as I began to have something more positive to focus on: my students. As the burdens began to get progressively lighter, I also experienced spiritual reprieve as the Holy Spirit continued to move upon me by giving me prophetic messages for those I came in contact with. During this time, there was one thing that I found to be so amazing and so refreshing: when I concentrate on the assignments that He places into my hands, my troubles seem to be so far away. Also, when I focus on God's business, I move out of His way, so that He can work miracles on my behalf.

During the continued undesirable course of events, the Holy Spirit brought many people before me in visions and in dreams and gave me messages for them. As I went about my way delivering God's message to each and every one of them, I began to feel refreshed and renewed even though my personal release had not manifested in the natural. I was letting God have His way by continuing to develop me in my office as His prophet.

During this time, not only did I deliver God's prophetic messages of confirmation, but His words of prophesy were delivered unto me as well. I had a least four prophets who came to me with similar messages. Their messages are paraphrased below:

Prophet #1: *"God has set you apart. He does not want everyone around you. He is doing that for a specific reason. Don't you know that the devil wants to take your life?"*

Prophet #2: *"Every time you take 3 or 4 steps forward and everything is going well and it seems as though nothing can touch you, something always pulls you back. It is like a yoke around your neck and there are strongholds. When you are going through these moments, you never lose your faith, but you do question whether or not God is testing you. That's not what it is. There are people praying against you. I don't know where you are going but there are some people who don't want to see you get there."*

Prophet #3: *"You are going to be able to see clearly again. God is going to wake you up between 2 and 6 in the morning, and you will see a cloud of mist. When He wakes you up, get on your knees and begin praying. He is going to answer your prayers. Be careful who you let get close to you. Be careful who you connect with. I am reminded of the story of Abraham and Lot. When Lot left, Abraham could hear from God. Where you are going, others can't go."*

Prophet #4: *"God is keeping you separate from everyone so that when He gives you a word they will know that it isn't coming from you but it is coming directly from the throne of Grace. They will know that the words you say are what 'thus saith the Lord.'"*

These God-sent comments gave me hope and would momentarily lift the cloud of depression that was unwilling to quickly dissipate. Because of the cloud's unwillingness to dissipate, I had to find a remedy for my situation. With all that I was experiencing, the only way I could see myself regaining clear thinking was to write. As a result, this book, **Through the Storm,** was birthed out. Its primary purposes were to serve as a healing process for me first and then for the readers of the book second.

Before we fully examine causes of depression and remedies, let us examine characters from the bible to learn about other instances of depression, their causes, and the results. When one surveys the bible, he/she will see issues of depression illuminated, even with some of the most famous bible characters. Let us look at King Saul for example. In the book of 1 Samuel, after Saul began his reign as king, a change came over him. He was no longer the God-fearing individual that he had once been. He began to take matters into his own hands and no longer consulted God for his instruction. After continuously failing to follow God's orders, when Saul's army defeated the Amalekites, Saul took King Agag and his soldiers for his very own prisoners. This was a direct violation of God's orders because King Saul was ordered to kill everyone and to retain nothing for himself. However, being rebellious, he chose to do otherwise.

As an immediate result, the next day the prophet Samuel, who had anointed Saul as king, found Saul, who greeted him saying, "I have performed the commandment of the LORD." Samuel answered, "If you obeyed the LORD, what are all these animals here for?" Saul made excuses, but Samuel was firm against all his arguments, pointing out that even if Saul sacrificed all those animals, as his excuse claimed, it wouldn't undo his act of rebellion. Obedience is precious to God. 1 Samuel 15:22 says, "Behold, to obey is better than sacrifice."

After trying to reason with Saul, Samuel turned to leave, realizing that there was no point in supporting Saul's regime further. But it would have been very embarrassing for Saul if Samuel didn't show his support. Saul begged Samuel to stay, and finally grabbed him by his robe, tearing it. This was a huge faux pas. Samuel replied, "The LORD has similarly torn the kingdom from you, and won't change his mind." Still, Saul begged Samuel not to embarrass him by leaving without saying a few appropriate words.

Samuel demanded a sword, which was brought to him. His appropriate words were addressed to the Amalekite King Agag: "As your sword has made women childless, so shall your mother be childless" — and he killed him, as the LORD had told Saul to do. Samuel went home, grieving deeply for a long time over the loss of Saul, who would eventually be replaced as king. They never saw each other again. In a private ceremony, the prophet Samuel, acting under God's direction, anointed an obscure boy named David to be the future king of Israel.

Ever since Samuel disavowed Saul, Saul had severe bouts of depression. His staff recommended music to sooth his mood, and so

David, a skilled harpist and singer, was retained as Saul's private musician. David was also a courageous young man who mixed well with Saul's military staff. Later, after the Israelites were constantly being threatened by the Philistines, David defeated Goliath and freed the Israelites from the threat of the Philistines. From this individual and courageous act, David gained fame. When King Saul got wind of this, he became jealous of David and more depression ensued.

To bring an end to the threat that King Saul unnecessarily felt from David, who had great respect for him, King Saul made many attempts to end David's life. David, in an attempt to save his life, fled. Finally, after committing a variety of destructive acts, King Saul decided to see what assistance he could get from a soothsayer, since God had refused to respond to him. He was hoping that this final act would give him peace. In doing so, it would also bring an end to his suffering of depression. All his attempts failed.

From the reading of Saul's account, we can see that depression *can* stem from disobedience and jealousy. In Saul's case, he never returned to the Lord to repent of his wrong doings. As a result, his life ended in turmoil, as he took his own life by falling on his sword after the Israelites were defeated by the Philistines. However, Saul's case is not demonstrative of all cases; not everyone suffers from depression because of disobedience and/or jealousy. Every person has to determine his/her own root cause of depression as well as his/her own healing process. Each person needs to discover a healthy technique for dealing with depression, one that will actually cause healing to manifest and not solicit other problems.

Other examples of depression in the bible include, but are not limited to:

Elijah- He asked that his life be taken because of fatigue and depression as he found himself fleeing from Jezebel after her threat to end Elijah's life (1 Kings 19). However, God still had work for his prophet to do. In completing the work of the Lord, Elijah's depression was extinguished as the Lord protected him from all hurt, harm and danger. After Elijah completed all of his assignments as commanded by the Lord, He was taken up to heaven in a whirlwind by a chariot with horses of fire, never to be seen on earth again.

Jonah- In the book of Jonah, the prophet Jonah knew that the Assyrians were a strong but vile nation who in his opinion deserved to be destroyed by God's wrath. He also knew that because God is a merciful and gracious God He would have mercy on the people of Nineveh if they repented and turned from their wicked ways. Therefore, when God commanded that he go and tell the inhabitants of Nineveh that they were to be destroyed if they failed to repent of their evil doings, he ran in the other direction. Eventually, after much turmoil and grief, Jonah obeyed the voice of the Lord. Afterwards, because Nineveh was not getting its just due, in Jonah's opinion, he became angry and went to sit under a tree in the sun to die because God had chosen to spare them (Jonah 4:1-6). Even though God fully exercised His right to forgive and He did not agree with Jonah's anger, He allowed a large leaf to grow over Jonah's head to protect him from the scorching sun. Later, he caused the leaf to die and leave Jonah exposed to the sun. With this act, God was showing Jonah that he should not be depressed over things he has no control over. He should be concerned with doing what is right and not worried about whom God shows favor to.

Naomi- When Naomi returned to Bethlehem, after being away for some time and after the death of her husband and two sons, she was warmly greeted by the women there. When they addressed her as Naomi, she told them to call her Mara which means "bitter" because God had dealt with her bitterly by taking the family away that He had blessed her with (Ruth 1:20-21). However, upon Naomi's return to Bethlehem, she brought in her accompaniment one of her daughter-in-laws, Ruth. Ruth eventually married Boaz, one of Ruth's wealthy kinsmen, and they produced a family. God restored the family that Naomi had thought was taken from her for good (The Book of Ruth). This act of God's kindness brought Naomi much happiness.

Jeremiah- Jeremiah said he regretted ever being born. In Jeremiah chapter twenty verses 7-10, Jeremiah makes his complaints to God. He is severely depressed about the outcomes of his service to God. He prophesies and no one listens. He urged the people of Judah to act and no one budged. He was poor, thrown in prison, and was taken to Egypt against his will. In all, Jeremiah was ill treated as a servant of God. But even in his depression, he did not really desire to turn from the hand of God. However, in verses 14-18, Jeremiah asks that his life be taken and questions why he was born at all. Of course, his request is not granted because the Lord still had work for Jeremiah to do. Even through the book of Lamentations, Jeremiah served as God's prophet even though he wept his way through. Those tears were not for himself; rather, they were for those who faced eminent destruction. As hard as his tasks were, God saw Jeremiah through and Jeremiah proved himself worthy.

Hannah- She was depressed for years because she was barren and could not give her husband children (1 Samuel 1:7:15). Hannah's husband's other wife Peninnah berated her constantly because of her inability to bare their husband any offspring. This caused Hannah to be severely depressed, which induced an overflow of tears and a loss of appetite. But she knew that the God that she served was a miracle-working God, so she prayed earnestly that God would open up her womb and allow her to conceive and give birth to a son. In return, Hannah promised to dedicate him to the service of the Lord. Her depression was subsequently released because her request was granted. In her joy, Hannah kept her promise and dedicated her son Samuel to the service of the Lord (1 Samuel 1:24-28).

From surveying the variety of accounts of depression from God's Holy Word, we can see that depression has many causes as well as many cures. In an effort to assist you, the readers of this book who may battle depression, I did some research on how to extinguish depression in a healthy manner from one's life. Here are my findings.

First, let us identify the symptoms of depression. Symptoms can range from moodiness, irritability, loss or increase of appetite, wanting to be alone, and feeling worthless, misunderstood and/or unloved to name a few.

To overcome these symptoms of depression the first thing you should do is pray. After praying, consider also doing the following:

1. Be in the present:

   When a thought train begins or when you find that a thought train carries you away causing you to dwell on past hurts, intentionally come back to the present and look at a tree or beautiful or interesting scene in the present and think about it.

2. Analyze:

Get the facts and analyze them to see whether your worry is well founded. In many cases, you will find that you are worrying for nothing. Also, if it is a problem with an emotional factor, you will benefit very much from looking at it from an outsider's perspective, or even in the perspective of some other person. Another way is to look at the problem from a future point of time. You will find changed dimensions of the problem by looking at it this way.

3. Think positively:

Positive ideas and constructive thoughts have great power, while negative ideas and destructive thinking poison your mind. Whenever you find that you are slipping into negative thoughts, make a conscious effort to replace them with positive thoughts and positive feelings.

4. Become Engaged.

It is often told that an idle mind is the devil's workshop. An idle mind is just like a monkey, moving to unnecessary places. But if you engage yourselves in activities, your worries are forgotten and you are better off. Find a hobby or creative activity which will detract you from your worries.

5. Don't get isolated.

Talk to other people, not about your worries but about them, their plans and their views. Also assume the role of a patient hearer. When you find that you are sharing their problems and trying to solve them, your view will be changing from a worried man or woman to a problem solver. Also you may find that your worries are petite compared to their real problems!!

Warning: Never use intoxication as a solution for your worries. It will increase the depression and also cause more damage (Meditation is Easy.com, 2006).

Now that we know what to do about depression, for those of you who suffer from depression, utter a word of prayer to obtain assistance from our heavenly father in removing the cloud that hovers overhead.

Precious Lord,

I come before you with a heavy heart full of despair. But I always know that I can turn to you for comfort. Father, if I have done anything that was not in your will that has caused this cloud to envelop me, please forgive me and wipe the slate clean. My desire is to always be in your will. Lord, please give me the strength to persevere throughout this journey. I know that you have called me for a mighty work and that you will direct my paths. Father, I am leaning on your everlasting arms, seeking comfort, peace, and your guidance. Right now Lord, I feel lost in an abyss that has encircled itself around me. Lord, help me to see clearly. You told me in your word that if I seek, I will find. If I knock, the door will be opened. If I ask, I shall receive. I am seeking; I am knocking; and I am asking. Father, I stand on the promises that you have given me in your word. And I profess that I will receive all that you have promised me. I believe that you will remove this cloud. I believe that I will gain strength to carry on and persevere. I believe that I will make it to my destiny's end. I believe that all will be better and that I will stand victorious. I thank you for working miracles on my behalf. I thank you for your many blessings, in the name of Jesus.

Amen

How can I help someone I love?

There may be some of you who may be witnessing someone battling depression. If you are, there is something you can do to help. The bible tells us, *"Heaviness in the heart of man maketh it stoop: but a good word maketh it glad"* Proverbs 12:25. *"Hope deferred maketh the heart sick: but when the desire cometh, it is a tree of life"* Proverbs 13:12. Daily, we go about healing the sick as they come into the church. We even make visits to those in hospitals and convalescent homes. But what about those that are sick in our very midst who fellowship with us daily? We must care for those who are amongst us as well as those who are not. We cannot continue to let the silent killer of depression linger. We must minister healing to the saints.

When you have tried to help someone else, you may have felt helpless to do anything because nothing you have done so far has worked. You may have tried to talk them out of it, pray them out of it, or maybe even shake them out of it. You may have thrown your hands up in despair, yet I say to you...do not despair. You have tools available to you that can help the depressed. You can offer them comfort, offer them faith, offer them hope, and offer them love. They may be hard pressed to find any of these things within themselves, but it is there. It is in them and it is in you. How good is a word "fitly spoken?" It is not so much what you say as it is when you say it. God will guide you...let Him lead you. And if you do not have anything good to say then quite bluntly, you are more help by saying nothing at all. Silent support triumphs over wasted words any day. Patiently endure the "night season" with them and together you will rejoice again in the light.

Here is a prayer for you.

Father God,

I come before you today because I desire to help those who are suffering from the silent killer of depression. Father, I know that this is not your design because your word says in 3 John 2 that you wish above all things that we may prosper and be in health, even as our soul prospers. So, Father I know that it is not your desire that your children perish from this dis-ease. So Father, on their behalf, I intercede and ask that you would work a miracle to change their situations. I come to you as a willing vessel asking if there is anything that you would have me to do or say that would minister healing, hope, and peace. Father, I ask also that you direct my paths by ordering my steps. Thank you, Lord for allowing me the opportunity to be used of you and to help my fellow brethren.

In the name of Jesus' I pray,

Amen.

Scriptures for Depression

Psalm 34:17 *The righteous cry, and the Lord heareth, and delivereth them out of all their troubles.*

Psalm 30:5 *For his anger endureth but a moment; in his favour is life: weeping may endure for a night, but joy cometh in the morning.*

Psalm 147:3 *He healeth the broken in heart, and bindeth up their wounds.*

Isaiah 43:2 *When thou passest through the waters, I will be with thee; and through the rivers, they shall not overflow thee: when thou walkest through the fire, thou shalt not be burned; neither shall the flame kindle upon thee.*

Isaiah 61:3 *To appoint unto them that mourn in Zion, to give unto them beauty for ashes, the oil of joy for mourning, the garment of praise for the spirit of heaviness; that they might be called trees of righteousness, the planting of the Lord, that he might be glorified.*

Isaiah 40:31 *But they that wait upon the Lord shall renew their strength; they shall mount up with wings as eagles; they shall run, and not be weary; and they shall walk, and not faint.*

Isaiah 41:10 *Fear thou not; for I am with thee: be not dismayed; for I am thy God: I will strengthen thee; yea, I will help thee; yea, I will uphold thee with the right hand of my righteousness.*

Isaiah 51:11 *Therefore the redeemed of the Lord shall return, and come with singing unto Zion; and everlasting joy shall be upon their head: they shall obtain gladness and joy; and sorrow and mourning shall flee away.*

Nehemiah 8:10 *Then he said unto them, Go your way, eat the fat, and drink the sweet, and send portions unto them for whom nothing is prepared: for this day is holy unto our Lord: neither be ye sorry; for the joy of the Lord is your strength.*

Romans 8:38-39 *For I am persuaded, that neither death, nor life, nor angels, nor principalities, nor powers, nor things present, nor things to come, nor height, nor depth, nor any other creature, shall be able to separate us from the love of God, which is in Christ Jesus our Lord.*

2 Corinthians 1:3-4 *Blessed be God, even the Father of our Lord Jesus Christ, the Father of mercies, and the God of all comfort; Who comforteth us in all our tribulation, that we may be able to comfort them which are in any trouble, by the comfort wherewith we ourselves are comforted of God.*

Philippians 4:8 *Finally, brethren, whatsoever things are true, whatsoever things are honest, whatsoever things are just, whatsoever things are pure, whatsoever things are lovely, whatsoever things are of good report; if there be any virtue, and if there be any praise, think on these things.*

Luke 18:1 *And he spake a parable unto them to this end, that men ought always to pray, and not to faint.*

1 Peter 4:12-13 *Beloved, think it not strange concerning the fiery trial which is to try you, as though some strange thing happened unto you: But rejoice, inasmuch as*

ye are partakers of Christ's sufferings; that, when his glory shall be revealed, ye may be glad also with exceeding joy.

Glimmers of Hope

The Old Man and the Dog

"Jody, Watch out! You nearly broad-sided that car!" My father yelled at me. "Can't you do anything right?" Those words hurt worse than blows. I turned my head toward the elderly man in the seat beside me, daring me to challenge him. A lump rose in my throat as I averted my eyes. I wasn't prepared for another battle. "I saw the car, Dad. Please don't yell at me when I'm driving." My voice was measured and steady, sounding far calmer than I really felt. Dad glared at me, then turned away and settled back.

At home, I left Dad in front of the television and went outside to collect my thoughts Dark, heavy clouds hung in the air with a promise of rain. The rumble of distant thunder seemed to echo my inner turmoil. What could I do about him? Dad had been a lumberjack in Washington and Oregon. He had enjoyed being outdoors and had reveled in pitting his strength against the forces of nature. He had entered grueling lumberjack competitions and had placed often. The shelves in his house were filled with trophies that attested to his prowess.

The years marched on relentlessly. The first time he couldn't lift a heavy log, he joked about it; but later that same day I saw him outside alone, straining to lift it. He became irritable whenever anyone teased him about his advancing age, or when he couldn't do something he had done as a younger man.

Four days after his sixty-seventh birthday, he had a heart attack. An ambulance sped him to the hospital while a paramedic administered

CPR to keep blood and oxygen flowing. At the hospital, Dad was rushed into an operating room.

He was lucky; he survived. But something inside Dad died. His zest for life was gone. He obstinately refused to follow doctor's orders. Suggestions and offers of help were turned aside with sarcasm and insults. The number of visitors thinned; then they finally stopped altogether. Dad was left alone.

My husband, Rick, and I asked Dad to come live with us on our small farm. We hoped the fresh air and rustic atmosphere would help him adjust. Within a week after he moved in, I regretted the invitation. It seemed nothing was satisfactory. He criticized everything I did. I became frustrated and moody. Soon I was taking my pent-up anger out on Rick. We began to bicker and argue. Alarmed, Rick sought out our pastor and explained the situation. The clergyman set up weekly counseling appointments for us. At the close of each session he prayed, asking God to soothe Dad's troubled mind. But the months wore on and God was silent. A raindrop struck my cheek as I looked up into the gray sky. Somewhere up there was "God."

Although I believe a Supreme Being had created the universe, I had difficulty believing that God cared about the tiny human beings on this earth. I was tired of waiting for a God who did not answer. Something had to be done and it was up to me to do it. The next day, I sat down with the phone book and methodically called each of the mental health clinics listed in the Yellow Pages. I explained my problem in vain to each of the sympathetic voices that answered. Just when I was giving up hope, one of the voices suddenly exclaimed, "I just read something that might help you! Let me go get the article." I listened as she read. The article described a remarkable study done at a nursing home. All of the patients were under treatment for chronic depression. Yet their attitudes had improved dramatically when they were given responsibility for a dog. I drove to the animal shelter that afternoon.

After I filled out a questionnaire, a uniformed officer led me to the kennels. The odor of disinfectant stung my nostrils as I moved down the row of pens. Each contained five to seven dogs. Long-haired dogs, curly-haired dogs, black dogs, spotted dogs - all jumped up, trying to reach me. I studied each one but rejected one after the other for various reasons, too big, too small, too much hair. As I neared the last pen, a dog in the shadows of the far corner struggled to his feet, walked to the front of the run and sat down. It was a pointer, one of the dog world's aristocrats. But this was a caricature of the breed.

Years had etched his face and muzzle with shades of gray. His hipbones jutted out in lopsided triangles. But it was his eyes that caught and held my attention. Calm and clear, they beheld me unwaveringly. I pointed to the dog. "Can you tell me about him?" The officer looked; then he shook his head in puzzlement. "He's a funny one that appeared out of nowhere and sat in front of the gate. We brought him in, figuring someone would be right down to claim him. That was two weeks ago and we've heard nothing. His time is up tomorrow." He gestured helplessly.

As the words sank in, I turned to the man in horror. "You mean you're going to kill him?"

"Ma'am," he said gently, "that's our policy. We don't have room for every unclaimed dog." I looked at the pointer again. The calm brown eyes awaited my decision. "I'll take him," I said. I drove home with the dog on the front seat beside me. When I reached the house, I honked the horn twice. I was helping my prize out of the car when Dad shuffled onto the front porch.

"Ta-da! Look what I got for you, Dad!" I said excitedly. Dad looked, then wrinkled his face in disgust. "If I had wanted a dog, I would have gotten one. And I would have picked out a better specimen than that bag of bones. Keep it! I don't want it." Dad waved his arm scornfully and turned back toward the house. Anger rose inside me. It squeezed together my throat muscles and pounded into my temples. "You'd better get used to him, Dad. He's staying!" Dad ignored me. "Did you hear me, Dad?" I screamed.

At those words, Dad whirled angrily, his hands clenched at his sides, his eyes narrowed and blazing with hate. We stood glaring at each other like duelists, when suddenly the pointer pulled free from my grasp. He wobbled toward my dad and sat down in front of him. Then slowly, carefully, he raised his paw. Dad's lower jaw trembled as he stared at the uplifted paw. Confusion replaced the anger in his eyes. The pointer waited patiently. Then Dad was on his knees hugging the animal. It was the beginning of a warm and intimate friendship. Dad named the pointer Cheyenne. Together he and Cheyenne explored the community.

They spent long hours walking down dusty lanes. They spent reflective moments on the banks of streams, angling for tasty trout. They even started to attend Sunday services together, Dad sitting in a pew and Cheyenne lying quietly at his feet. Dad and Cheyenne were inseparable throughout the next three years. Dad's bitterness faded, and he and Cheyenne made many friends. Then late one night, I was startled to feel Cheyenne's cold nose burrowing through our bed covers. He had never before come into our bedroom at night. I woke Rick, put on my robe and ran into my father's room. Dad lay in his bed, his face serene; but his spirit had left quietly sometime during the night.

Two days later, my shock and grief deepened when I discovered Cheyenne lying dead beside Dad's bed. I wrapped his still form in the rag rug he had slept on. As Rick and I buried him near a favorite fishing hole, I silently thanked the dog for the help he had given me in restoring Dad's peace of mind.

The morning of Dad's funeral dawned overcast and dreary. This day looks like the way I feel, I thought, as I walked down the aisle to the pews reserved for family. I was surprised to see the many friends Dad and Cheyenne had made filling the church. The pastor began his eulogy. It was a tribute to both Dad and the dog who had changed his life. And then the pastor turned to Hebrews 13:2. "Be not forgetful to entertain strangers..." "I've often thanked God for sending that angel," he said.

For me, the past dropped into place, completing a puzzle that I had not seen before: the sympathetic voice that had just read the right article ~ Cheyenne's unexpected appearance at the animal shelter ~ His calm acceptance and complete devotion to my father ~ and the proximity of their deaths. And suddenly I understood.

I knew that God had answered my prayers after all.

~by Catherine Moore~

Hope is Not Lost

One day a while back, a man, his heart heavy with grief, was walking in the woods. As he thought about his life this day, he knew many things were not right. He thought about those who had lied about him back when he had a job. His thoughts turned to those who had stolen his things and cheated him. He remembered family that had passed on. His mind turned to the illness he had, that no one could cure. His very soul was filled with anger, resentment, and frustration.

Standing there this day, searching for answers he could not find, knowing all else had failed him, he knelt at the base of an old oak tree to seek the one he knew would always be there. And with tears in his eyes, he prayed: 'Lord- You have done wonderful things for me in this life. You have told me to do many things for you, and I happily obeyed. Today, you have told me to forgive. I am sad, Lord, because I cannot; I don't know how. It is not fair Lord; I didn't deserve these wrongs that were done against me and I shouldn't have to forgive. As perfect as your way is Lord, this one thing I cannot do, for I don't know how to forgive. My anger is so deep, Lord. I fear I may not hear you, but I pray you teach me to do the one thing I cannot do: teach me to forgive.'

As he knelt there in the quiet shade of that old oak tree, he felt something fall onto his shoulder. He opened his eyes. Out of the corner of one eye, he saw something red on his shirt. He could not turn to see what it was because where the oak tree had been was a large square piece of wood in the ground. He raised his head and saw two feet held to the wood with a large spike through them.

He raised his head more, and tears came to his eyes as he saw Jesus hanging on a cross. He saw spikes in His hands, a gash in His side, a torn and battered body, and deep thorns sunk into His head. Finally, he saw the suffering and pain on His precious face. As their eyes met, the man's tears turned to sobbing, and Jesus began to speak.

'Have you ever told a lie?' he asked.

The man answered - 'Yes, Lord.'

'Have you ever been given too much change and kept it?'

The man answered - 'Yes. Lord.' And the man sobbed more and more.

'Have you ever taken something from work that wasn't yours?' Jesus asked.

And the man answered, 'Yes, Lord.'

'Have you ever sworn, using my Father's name in vain?'

The man, crying now, answered - 'Yes, Lord.'

As Jesus asked many more times, 'Have you ever'? The man's crying became uncontrollable, for he could only answer - 'Yes, Lord'.

Then Jesus turned His head from one side to the other, and the man felt something fall on his other shoulder. He looked and saw that it was the blood of Jesus. When he looked back up, his eyes met those of Jesus, and there was a look of love the man had never seen or known before.

Jesus said, 'I didn't deserve this either, but I forgive you.'

It may be hard to see how you're going to get through something, but when you look back in life, you realize how true this statement is.

Read the following first line slowly and let it sink in.

If God brings you to it - He will bring you through it.

When Jesus died on the cross, he was thinking of you!

A Friend Indeed

One day, when I was a freshman in high school, I saw a kid from my class walking home from school. His name was Kyle. It looked like he was carrying all of his books. I thought to myself, "Why would anyone bring home all his books on a Friday? He must really be a nerd." I had quite a weekend planned (parties and a football game with my friends tomorrow afternoon), so I shrugged my shoulders and went on.

As I was walking, I saw a bunch of kids running toward him. They ran at him, knocking all his books out of his arms and tripping him so he landed in the dirt.

His glasses went flying, and I saw them land in the grass about ten feet from him. He looked up and I saw this terrible sadness in his eyes. My heart went out to him. So, I jogged over to him, and as he crawled around looking for his glasses, I saw a tear in his eye.

As I handed him his glasses, I said, "Those guys are jerks. They really should get lives." He looked at me and said, "Hey thanks!" There was a big smile on his face. It was one of those smiles that showed real gratitude. I helped him pick up his books and asked him where he lived. As it turned out, he lived near me, so I asked him why I had never seen him before. He said he had gone to private school before now. I would have never hung out with a private school kid before.

We talked all the way home, and I carried some of his books. He turned out to be a pretty cool kid. I asked him if he wanted to play a little football with my friends. He said yes. We hung out all weekend and the more I got to know Kyle, the more I liked him, and my friends thought the same of him. Monday morning came, and there was Kyle with the huge stack of books again. I stopped him and said, "Boy, you are gonna really build some serious muscles with this pile of books everyday!" He just laughed and handed me half the books. Over the next four years, Kyle and I became best friends.

When we were seniors, we began to think about college. Kyle decided on Georgetown, and I was going to Duke. I knew that we would always be friends, that the miles would never be a problem. He was going to be a doctor, and I was going for business on a football scholarship. Kyle was valedictorian of our class. I teased him all the time about being a nerd. He had to prepare a speech for graduation. I was so glad it wasn't me having to get up there and speak. Graduation day, I saw Kyle. He looked great. He was one of those guys that really found himself during high school.

He filled out and actually looked good in glasses. He had more dates than I had and all the girls loved him. Boy, sometimes I was jealous! Today was one of those days. I could see that he was nervous about his speech. So, I smacked him on the back and said, "Hey, big guy, you'll be great!" He looked at me with one of those looks (the really grateful one) and smiled. "Thanks," he said. As he started his speech, he cleared his throat and began. "Graduation is a time to thank those who helped you make it through those tough years. Your parents, your teachers, your siblings, maybe a coach...but mostly your friends... I am here to tell all of you that being a friend to someone is the best gift you can give them. I am going to tell you a story." I just looked at my friend with disbelief as he told the story of the first day we met. He had planned to kill himself over the weekend. He talked of how he had cleaned out his locker so his mom wouldn't have to do it later and was carrying his stuff home.

He looked hard at me and gave me a little smile. "Thankfully, I was saved. My friend saved me from doing the unspeakable." I heard the gasp go through the crowd as this handsome, popular boy told us all about his weakest moment. I saw his mom and dad looking at me and smiling that same grateful smile. Not until that moment did I realize its depth.

Never underestimate the power of your actions. With one small gesture, you can change a person's life. For better or for worse.

Defining One's Self

A young woman went to her mother and told her about her life and how things were so hard for her. She did not know how she was going to make it and wanted to give up. She was tired of fighting and struggling. It seemed as one problem was solved, a new one arose.

Her mother took her to the kitchen. She filled three pots with water and placed each on a high fire. Soon, the pots came to boil. In the first, she placed carrots; in the second, she placed eggs; and in the last, she placed ground coffee beans. She let them sit and boil, without saying a word.

After about twenty minutes, she turned off the burners. She fished the carrots out and placed them in a bowl. She pulled the eggs out and placed them in a bowl. Then she ladled the coffee out and placed it in a bowl. Turning to her daughter, she asked, "Tell me what you see." "Carrots, eggs, and coffee," she replied.

Her mother brought her closer and asked her to feel the carrots.

She did and noted that they were soft. The mother then asked the daughter to take an egg and break it. After pulling off the shell, she observed the hard boiled egg. Finally, the mother asked the daughter to sip the coffee. The daughter smiled as she tasted its rich aroma. The daughter then asked, "What does it mean, mother?"

Her mother explained that each of these objects had faced the same adversity: boiling water. Each reacted differently. The carrot went in strong, hard, and unrelenting. However, after being subjected to the boiling water, it softened and became weak. The egg had been fragile. Its thin outer shell had protected its liquid interior, but after sitting through the boiling water, its inside became hardened. The ground coffee beans were unique, however. After they were in the boiling water, they had changed the water.

"Which are you?" she asked her daughter. "When adversity knocks on your door, how do you respond? Are you a carrot, an egg or a coffee bean?

Think of this: Which am I? Am I the carrot that seems strong, but with pain and adversity do I wilt and become soft and lose my strength? Am I the egg that starts with a malleable heart, but changes with the heat? Did I have a fluid spirit, but after a death, a breakup, a financial hardship or some other trial, have I become hardened and stiff? Does my shell look the same, but on the inside am I bitter and tough with a stiff spirit and hardened heart? Or am I like the coffee bean? The bean actually changes the hot water, the very circumstance that brings the pain. When the water gets hot, it releases the fragrance and flavor. If you are like the bean, when things are at their worst, you get better and change the situation around you. When the hour is the darkest and trials are their greatest, do you elevate yourself to another level? How do you handle adversity? Are you a carrot, an egg or a coffee bean?

May you have enough happiness to make you sweet, enough trials to make you strong, enough sorrow to keep you human and enough hope to make you happy.

The happiest of people don't necessarily have the best of everything; they just make the most of everything that comes along their way. The brightest future will always be based on a forgotten past; you can't go forward in life until you let go of your past failures and heartaches.

Two

Education Gone Amiss

Have you ever had a dream of completing a course at school, obtaining a degree, license or certificate? As a child, all I ever wanted to do professionally was teach. Since I was seven or eight years old, I have had a craving to impart knowledge to others, and I was and still am very emphatic about it. When ever anyone asked what I wanted to be when I grew up, I would stand proudly, with my shoulders squared and my flat chest puffed up, and I would enthusiastically say, "I *am going* to be a teacher!" not I *want* to be a teacher. Everyone in my family from my mother, to my brothers, grandmother, aunts, and cousins knew that I was to become a teacher. And I would be the first in my family. It was my destiny. It is what God called me to do before I departed from my mother's womb.

So, in an effort to attain my goal and fulfill God's calling, after high school I set out to go to college and earn a bachelor's degree so that I could enter into an elementary classroom to teach in an official capacity. I say in an official capacity because I actually started teaching in third grade, but that is all together a different story that I could tell you. After earning my degree and teaching for several years, I opted to further my education by earning a master's degree. The question, at that point, was in what field I wanted to pursue my master's degree.

I decided to look over my transcript and see what type of degree I could pursue that would take the normal two-year time frame. As a result, I discovered that I had enough courses in English to pursue a degree in English Composition. However, because my bachelor's degree was not in English, I did have to take more undergraduate English courses in addition to my graduate courses in order to complete my degree. The positive side of that was that I could take courses concurrently and get finished in a decent amount of time. So, I worked hard by taking three courses a quarter while being a divorced mother of two sons and working part time. This rigid schedule enabled me to finish my master's degree in English Composition. Once my degree was complete, I decided to move up from teaching high school English to teaching English at the college level, where eight years later, I still teach today.

As time went on, I began to write, edit, and publish my own books. During that span of time, many people have posed the question of why I decided to master in English and why I decided to write. At first, out of my ignorance, I would explain to them that my degree in English was by default because it would take too long to pursue a degree in math, which was and still is my favorite subject. Later, though, I discovered that my mastering in English was not by default but by God's divine plan. He set me on this course for a purpose, which is to feed His sheep His word through the written form. To testify to this statement, all of my spiritual-based books have been and will always be guided by the Holy Spirit. I write what He tells me to write, period.

Okay, so much for two successful degrees. The time came when I decided to pursue the highest, terminal and elitist degree- the Ph. D., the doctorate. Well, for the first year all went well. I finished all the course work within one year. I took three courses at a time. The next stage was the exams. I had to pass the exams in order to continue in the program. If I failed the exams, I would be given only one additional opportunity to redo them. If I failed a second time, I would be expurgated from the program, never to return. Well, during the times of my exams I was faced with marital turmoil on a daily basis and unfortunately from not being able to devote my concerns and energy to my studies, I failed my exams.

I was totally devastated because in all my accomplishments and in all my trials and in all my disasters, I had never in my entire life failed anything (except for maybe a test in school that I had not prepared for). When I called my mother to tell her, initially she did not believe me. She thought I was joking because as I said I have never failed anything. I had to assure her that I was not joking, as I did not see this as a joking matter. It was one of the most difficult and heart-wrenching phone calls that I ever had to make, even at thirty-eight years old. I was livid with grief.

All I could do was cry and cry and cry some more. When I finished crying, I regrouped and I was ready to pursue the task of rewriting my exams. I had two weeks to do so. Just when I was ready to begin writing, my ulcer erupted, and my husband of a year and a half decided to leave home right in the middle of my rewrite time. That was also devastating. Not the fact that he left, but the fact that he didn't care if he disrupted my life any further during such a crucial time. Well, to God be the glory. After the two-week period for the rewrite, I had to wait another two weeks to get my results. I passed!!!!!!!!!

The third and final phase of the doctorate program is to conduct the research and compose the dissertation. During this final stage, I went through attempted reconciliation and finally divorce after a total of three years of marriage that was filled with heartache and turmoil. During this time, I had done more of nothing than writing. At the time this book was written, I had decided to take one term off from school and re-enter at the beginning of the following term which began at the beginning of the year, 2008. I figured I could regroup, continue my research, and get back on track. As I was preparing to refocus my attention on my dissertation, this book kept pulling at my heart. So the writing began.

I figured once the book had been written, I could and would refocus on my dissertation so I could graduate. For some of you who read this book, I will still be working to complete my degree while others will read it and my doctorate will have been completed. I praise God in advance for what He is doing and what He will do in my future. I know that He will order my steps in all that I do. Psalms 37:23 tells us that, *"The steps of a good man are ordered by the LORD: and he delighteth in his way."*

Some of you may be reading this and actually feel the disappointment of what I experienced, while others may be thinking that I have obtained many of my educational and career objectives and that I should be satisfied. Some may feel that I should not complain about troubles because many have not made it as far as I have and I should be grateful. Well, the truth is I am very grateful to my heavenly Father, for all He has done for me. I am content, but I am <u>not</u> satisfied. My heavenly Father promised me treasures here on earth, and I have set my heart to attain all that He has for me. I aim to drink in the very elixir of life and its fullness. I believe that everyone should reach his/her personal educational goals. For some, the goal may be earning a high school diploma after being out of school for 30 years. For others, it may be attaining a certificate in a particular field. For still others, it may be a specific degree that is needed for career advancement.

I believe that whatever a person's educational desire is, he/she should strive to attain it. We know that the bible says, *"My people are destroyed for lack of knowledge"* (Hosea 4:6). I am a firm believer that the bible is not only referring to knowledge of biblical principles. I believe that although we are not of this world, we must live in it and in order to function to our fullest capacity, we must be knowledgeable about earthly things. Therefore, in an effort to not perish from a lack of knowledge, we must equip ourselves with mental ammunition.

Although attending school and earning degrees is not for everyone, knowledge should be everyone's friend, and we should put our knowledge to work for us. Throughout the 31 chapters of Proverbs, Solomon constantly reminds us to not be a fool because, "*A fool's talk brings a rod to his back, but the lips of the wise protect them*" (Proverbs 14:3). Solomon also tells us to, "*Stay away from a foolish man, for you will not find knowledge on his lips*" (Proverbs 14:7).

According to dictionary.net, a fool is, "One destitute of reason, or of the common powers of understanding; an idiot; a natural; 2. a person deficient in intellect; one who acts absurdly, or pursues a course contrary to the dictates of wisdom; one without judgment; a simpleton; a dolt; 3. one who acts contrary to moral and religious wisdom; a wicked person." Many agree with the first definition which states that a fool is someone who lacks common sense.

I prefer the third definition. From this definition and from Solomon's examples of the fool's behavior, a fool is not someone who lacks sound judgment or information. No, a fool is someone who is mentally capable of making sound decisions and, in most cases, has the information to do so, but chooses not to. A person who does not have sufficient information to make informed decisions on a topic is simply ignorant about the topic. One is considered to be ignorant when he/she lacks information. A fool, on the other hand, has the information and does not apply it.

So, it is time to hold up the stop sign for the enemy. Stop allowing him to lie to you about your being too old to go back to school. Stop letting him tell you that you cannot afford it. Stop allowing him to tell you that you are not smart enough. Education is not about being smart; it is about having endurance to finish the race. Trust me, *once* I questioned my ability to finish my doctorate, but I stopped myself and said, "Oh no! The devil is not going to lead me down the path of doubting myself. I am equipped and capable to finish the task." Some of you need to boldly declare the same thing.

Let's do a faith-building exercise. Repeat the following words that are taken from an excerpt by Marianne Williamson:

> Our deepest fear is not that we are inadequate. Our deepest fear is that we are powerful beyond measure. It is our light, not our darkness that most frightens us. We ask ourselves, "Who am I to be brilliant, gorgeous, talented, fabulous?" Actually, who are you *not* to be? You are a child of God. Your playing small does not serve the world. There is nothing enlightened about shrinking so that other people won't feel insecure around you. We are all meant to shine, as children do. We were born to make manifest the glory of God that is within us. It's not just in some of us; it's in everyone. And as we let our own light shine, we unconsciously give other people permission to

do the same. As we are liberated from our own fear, our presence automatically liberates others.

Now read it again, but this time, make it personal by referring to yourself. "My deepest fear is not that I am inadequate. My deepest fear….." Whenever you feel the spirit of fear creeping in to tell you what you cannot do, recite the words of Williamson's excerpt.

Like the words above, we want to speak life into our situations, regardless of what they look like on the outside. Always remember to utter affirmations rather than negative comments, for the bible tells us that, *"Death and life are in the power of the tongue"* (Proverbs 18:21). So even when the seemingly impossible faces us, we need to speak a word of faith.

Here is an example of a comment that on the surface appears to be realistic, but is actually a negative, debilitating comment. During a parent-teacher conference, a teacher told a student's mother that the child was having difficulty with math. The mother said, "I told my daughter that it was okay if she did not do well in math. I never did well either." I was taken completely aback by the absurd comment. I, just like most people, have studied the theory of heredity that discusses various traits being inherited through genes. I do believe in the carrying of genes from parent to child because that is the nature of our DNA. But we must remember that we are not carbon copies of our parents. We are not them and they are not us. Simply put, we are individuals who have our own genetic makeup that was indeed contributed by our parents. However, we are not our parents' clones. Also, there is such a thing as recessed genes. Recessed genes are genes that may not appear for a number of generations but suddenly appear after being recessed. Even more powerful than recessed genes or the makeup of our DNA is the power of God. We can be and do whatever He proclaims for our lives.

With that said, let's revisit the mother's comment. Telling the daughter that she should not expect to do well in mathematics is debilitating because the daughter may actually be very good at math but is having a difficult time understanding certain concepts at that moment. As a result of her mother's comment, she may never exert the proper energy to do well. This could have secondary effects. As a result of not doing well, she may then limit herself in making career decisions that are based incorrectly on her strengths or lack of strengths. As you can see, one comment can send a person down the wrong path.

It would have been better to tell the little girl that even though math may not be the easiest subject for her, with a little extra work she could learn the concepts. Later, if the girl decided that math was too strenuous for her and after applying herself to the best of her ability that she did not want to pursue higher levels of math or a career focused around math that is a choice that she is free to make. Parents and teachers, on the other hand, should not make choices for students, especially when they are in elementary school and their brains are still developing. We are to serve as guides and to assist in building strengths and weaknesses.

We can see this principle at work in the bible. In the book of Genesis, Moses did not believe that he could be God's chosen vessel to deliver the Israelites out of Egypt because of the weakness in his speech. But God did not emphasize his weakness. Instead, he focused on Moses' strengths. When given the assignment to lead the Israelites out of Egypt, Moses complained about his speech (Exodus 4:10). God insisted that since He made the mouth that it could and would do what He wanted it to do (v. 11) even when humans try to enforce limitations. But since Moses consistently complained, God came up with an alternative to Moses being the primary speaker. He decided to use Moses' brother Aaron as his mouthpiece (v. 16).

In the end, Moses still had to do what God called him to do. After all, it was not Moses' speech that God was interested in; it was his leadership skills. God knew that it took a strong leader to lead a group of that magnitude, one that the people would listen to and respect (for the most part). From this example, we learn that when God has a call on our lives, it is not up to us to figure out how it is going to be done. We need to learn to walk according to our purpose and let God lead us to and through it. This applies not only to education but to all areas of our lives.

If you have a desire to complete educational goals that you set for yourself and they seem to keep slipping from your grasp, pray the following prayer of request.

Father God,

I come to you in the name of Jesus Christ, my Lord and my Savior. I come to you today Lord to thank you for the opportunity that you have afforded me to obtain an education and I thank you that the opportunity is yet before me. Father, I pray that you will direct my paths and show me how to get from where I am now to where I want to go. Father, I request that you will bless me with the proper resources that will enable me to be a success in my educational endeavors. Father, I receive these blessings and I walk in educational victory.

In Jesus' name,

Amen

How can I help someone I love?

Maybe you read this chapter on education and you are saying that you are happy with your educational endeavors and God has richly blessed you in your efforts. Congratulations! But, I would venture to say that there is at least one person around you that does not share the same testimony. There are many people in our day-to-day environment who struggle with meeting their educational desires. Some lack resources for finding the school that will meet their schedules; others lack the finances they need; while still others struggle with issues of daycare for their young children. There are many things that you can do to assist someone who desires to advance his/her education.

First, of all, when helping others to meet their educational desires, we should listen attentively to their personal situation so we can see what the impediment is. Once we have heard their story, we will know where to place our efforts in assisting them in obtaining their goals. Over the course of twenty years, I have tried to assist many people in reaching their goals. Some make it and some do not. One thing that I had to learn was, you can lead a person to the school door, but you can not make them enter. You can lead them past the door, but you can not make them study. You can get them to take one class, but you can not make them complete a program. The ultimate choice is theirs. And I'm not referring to people who do not want to go to school. I am referring to those who say they really want to go but let obstacles prevent them from going. So, do not be discouraged if all your efforts seem to go down the drain. Do your part and let them do theirs.

Some things you can do to help is to go online and find out about financial aid that may be available to them; you can take them to the school of their choice and get the registration forms and show them how to choose classes; or you may even need to volunteer to be their babysitter once in a while. When I was working on my master's and I had to take evening classes, my friend Deeneice babysat my youngest son Daron after the daycare closed. Her assistance enabled me to take night classes after my evening classes.

Regardless of what area you choose to assist in, your help is needed. Some people do not know how to ask for help or maybe they are too proud or too embarrassed, but let the Good Samaritan in you come out and offer the assistance that they need. Sometimes having someone on a journey with you makes the road a lot easier to travel.

Here is a prayer for you.

Heavenly Father,

Thank you for all that you have done in my life and for all that you have blessed me with. Father, I desire to be a blessing to someone else. Let my light shine so that I may be a beacon of hope to others who desire to better themselves and to provide a better life for their families. Give me the courage to speak out and help others who may not be able to find their way. Let me be of assistance to them. Father, give me words of encouragement to give to them. Father, use me in a mighty way so that I may speak life in what appears to be a dead and hopeless situation. Thank you for trusting me Lord with this awesome task.

In Jesus' name,

Amen.

The following song was my theme song when I graduated with my masters and will be my theme song again when I graduate with my doctorate. Maybe it can serve as a source of inspiration for you.

"I Believe I Can Fly" by R. Kelly

I used to think that I could not go on
And life was nothing but an awful song
But now I know the meaning of true love
I'm leaning on the everlasting arms

If I can see it, then I can do it
If I just believe it, there's nothing to it

[1] - I believe I can fly
I believe I can touch the sky
I think about it every night and day
Spread my wings and fly away
I believe I can soar
I see me running through that open door
I believe I can fly
I believe I can fly
I believe I can fly

See I was on the verge of breaking down
Sometimes silence can seem so loud
There are miracles in life I must achieve
But first I know it starts inside of me, oh

If I can see it, then I can be it
If I just believe it, there's nothing to it

[Repeat 1]

Hey, cuz I believe in me, oh

Through the Storm   C. White-Elliott

If I can see it, then I can do it
If I just believe it, there's nothing to it

[Repeat 1]

Hey, if I just spread my wings
I can fly
I can fly
I can fly, hey
If I just spread my wings
I can fly
Fly-eye-eye

Glimmers of Hope

A Lesson Learned

A mom was concerned about her kindergarten son walking to school. He didn't want his mother to walk with him. She wanted to give him the feeling that he had some independence, but yet know that he was safe. So she had an idea of how to handle it.

She asked a neighbor, Mrs. Goodnest, if she would please follow him to school in the mornings, staying at a distance, so he probably wouldn't notice her. Mrs. Goodnest said that since she was up early with her toddler anyway, it would be a good way for them to get some exercise as well, so she agreed. The next school day, Mrs. Goodnest and her little girl, Marcy, set out following behind Timmy as he walked to school with another neighbor boy he knew. She did this for the whole week. As the boys walked and chatted, kicking stones and twigs, Timmy's little friend noticed the same lady was following them as she seemed to do every day all week.

Finally he said to Timmy, "Have you noticed that lady following us to school all week? Do you know her?" Timmy nonchalantly replied, "Yeah, I know who she is." The friend said, "Well, who is she?" "That's just Shirley Goodnest," Timmy replied, "and her daughter Marcy." "Shirley Goodnest? Who the heck is she and why is she following us?" "Well," Timmy explained, "Every night my mom makes me say the 23rd Psalm with my prayers, 'cuz she worries about me so much. And in the Psalm, it says 'Shirley Goodnest and Marcy shall follow me all the days of my life,' guess I'll just have to get used to it!"

This story, but cute, testimony demonstrates learning in both arenas-secular and the spiritual. Remember the verse, *"Train up a child in the way he should go; and when he is old, he will not depart from it"* (Proverbs 22:6).

Need Washing??

A little girl had been shopping with her mom in Target. She must have been 6 years old, this beautiful red haired, freckled-faced image of innocence. It was pouring outside. The kind of rain that gushes over the top of rain gutters, so much in a hurry to hit the earth it has no time to flow down the spout. We all stood there under the awning and just inside the door of the Target.

We waited, some patiently, others irritated because nature messed up their hurried day. I am always mesmerized by rainfall. I got lost in the sound and sight of the heavens washing away the dirt and dust of the world. Memories of running, splashing so carefree as a child came pouring in as a welcome reprieve from the worries of my day.

The little voice was so sweet as it broke the hypnotic trance we were all caught in, "Mom, let's run through the rain," she said.
"What?" Mom asked.
"Let's run through the rain!" she repeated.
"No, honey. We'll wait until it slows down a bit," Mom replied.

This young child waited about another minute and repeated: "Mom, let's run through the rain."

"We'll get soaked if we do," Mom said.

"No, we won't, Mom. That's not what you said this morning," the young girl said as she tugged at her mom's arm.

"This morning? When did I say we could run through the rain and not get wet?"

"Don't you remember? When you were talking to Daddy about his cancer, you said, 'If God can get us through this, he can get us through anything!'"

The entire crowd stopped dead silent. I swear you couldn't hear anything but the rain. We all stood silently. No one came or left in the next few minutes.

Mom paused and thought for a moment about what she would say. Now some would laugh it off and scold her for being silly. Some might even ignore what was said. But this was a moment of affirmation in a young child's life, a time when innocent trust can be nurtured so that it will bloom into faith. "Honey, you are absolutely right. Let's run through the rain. If GOD let's us get wet, well maybe we just needed washing," Mom said.

Then off they ran. We all stood watching, smiling and laughing as they darted past the cars and yes, through the puddles. They held their shopping bags over their heads just in case they got soaked. But they were followed by a few who screamed and laughed like children all the way to their cars. And yes, I did. I ran. I got wet. I needed washing.

Circumstances or people can take away your material possessions, they can take away your money, and they can take away your health.

But no one can ever take away your precious memories...So, don't forget to make time and take the opportunities to make memories everyday. To everything there is a season and a time to every purpose under heaven.

I HOPE YOU STILL TAKE THE TIME TO RUN THROUGH THE RAIN.

From the innocent reminders of children, we can learn how to live life a little more carefree.

Three

Putting Money in a Bag with a Hole

I am sure you have heard the not-so-endearing phrase "robbing Peter to pay Paul." That means you are taking money that was designed for one bill (Peter) to pay another one (Paul). Bishop Leon Martin, when teaching on managing finances, likes to say, "You rob Peter to pay Paul; what are you going to do when Peter and Paul show up at the same time? You will really have a serious problem." At this question and statement, the congregation laughs. But the reality of this "robbing" is not funny. At one time or another, many of us have found ourselves in this predicament, but we learn how to craftily juggle money and we make ends meet.

Just like many others, I have found myself in the juggling business. However, I can recall a time when I had to change the phrase from "robbing Peter to pay Paul" to "robbing Peter and Paul to pay Mary." I know, I know. Not good. But I must say Jehovah Jirah came to my rescue and my juggling act ceased. However, I also must admit that

He did not come when I wanted Him to, but what is important is that He came right on time. Hallelujah!!! Glory to God.

In the interim of my waiting period, my flesh was terrified that I was going to lose my home, my vehicle, and all the other earthly possessions that God had blessed me with. In my spirit, though, I kept saying, "I don't believe God would bless me with the desires of my heart just to take them away." But then, I know that God works in mysterious ways. For all I knew, there was something He wanted me to learn. I didn't know what, but I was willing to listen to Him and to learn any lessons He placed before me.

For days, weeks, and months, the agony of finances wore on me. It tore into my soul like a ferocious lion, which had not eaten in a month, does a leopard. It enveloped my being and became my daily focal point. I woke up thinking, "What can I do today to bring in additional income?" I went to bed thinking and asking, "Did I try hard enough? What could I have done differently? Tomorrow will be a better day. I hope."

The problem that I had was leaning to my own understanding. Even though I said I trusted God, my actions proved otherwise. I prayed and I fasted, but I still looked for methods that were within my immediate power to obtain the funds that I needed to take care of my expenses. It was not to say that I was wrong in doing that. I just seemed to go overboard. I did not know where to separate my physical abilities and allow my faith to kick in.

One thing that tore at me the most was to ask for assistance from friends and loved ones. I really wanted to work things out on my own. Actually, I just wanted God to work a miracle, and I wanted Him to do it expeditiously. Well, the time came when I decided to step around my pride and open my mouth to ask for assistance. Let's just say that when I did, I wished I had not. At the time, everyone seemed to be in the same financial predicament. Some were off work, while others were earnestly trying to save their homes as well. Others, I believe, did not believe that I really needed help. Some friends and family members seem to think I have a magic money tree. I guess they figured I would work everything out.

As time drew on, I began to discover that the overwhelming stress of it all would kill me. How would I enjoy my sons and our home, my job and my students, my church and my fellow brethren, and my family and friends if I were not here? Quite bluntly- I could not. At that moment, I had to re-learn and remember how to fully adhere to Proverbs 3:5-6, one of my favorite scriptures. It says, *"Trust in the LORD with all thine heart; and lean not unto thine own understanding. In all thy ways acknowledge him, and he shall direct thy paths."* I must say, adhering to this scripture is easier said than it is done.

Let me explain my difficulty. As an independent woman who is a self starter, a motivator, a single mother of two teenage sons, I have for most of my life had to find my own direction and make my own decisions and mistakes. To allow someone else, whether flesh or spirit, to come in and make decisions for me was extremely difficult. But I have learned to lean on the comforting shoulder of my heavenly father. My problem, however, is reverting back to the old woman who wants to find my own solutions and be independent. I had to learn that fully capitulating to and trusting in God does not make me any less of a woman. Actually it makes me more His woman than my own. It makes me His creation and not a mess that I created. Praise the Lord for that revelation!

In the midst of being refined, I had to ask myself, "With all the money problems that I am facing, am I putting my money into a bag that has a hole in it as said by the prophet Haggai, in Haggai 1:6?" "Have I neglected my service to the Lord and now I am suffering financially?" "Am I making unwise financial decisions with the money that is coming in?" "Am I digging a deeper hole for myself and my family?" These are the questions one should ask when faced with possible deleterious behaviors. Some of us may find that is not our spending or financial planning that is causing the problem. Rather, it may be the amount of income that is coming in versus the amount that is needed to go out. For others, it may be exorbitant spending practices that cause unforeseen financial distresses. And like in the book of Haggai, it may be a situation similar to the one where the people worked to build their own homes and gave no thought to the rebuilding of God's temple. Regardless of what category you find yourself in, it is the realization of the situation that will lend itself to finding the right solution.

If we look hard enough, we will find that God has already made provisions for us. We really need to seek Him because the answer that He will provide is unique to our personal situation. And when we discover the answer to our dilemma, the healthiest thing to do is not to beat ourselves up but to learn from our situations and move forward. What is done is in the past. Look toward a bright future. I did, and I walk in it today. 3 John 2 states, "*Beloved, I wish above all things that thou mayest prosper and be in health, even as thy soul prospereth.*" Here, we see that we are destined for prosperity in all areas of our life; this includes finances.

Now let us examine cases from the bible where we can learn how our view about money can affect our lives. The book of Matthew is filled with numerous instances of money issues. Many of these stories are shared by Jesus himself in the form of parables. Let's begin our survey in Matthew chapter six verses 19-21, where Jesus teaches about money. Here Jesus, as part of His Sermon on the Mount, tells the disciples not to store treasures on earth where they can be destroyed and/or stolen. He tells them to instead store their treasures in heaven where they will be protected. He warns us that where our treasures are our heart will be also, and he tells us that we cannot serve two masters. We must choose between serving God and serving money. Serving God has its rewards and pays better dividends.

In other biblical lessons about money, let us read to see who or what the participants chose to serve. In chapter fourteen verses 23-35, Jesus tells the story of the Unforgiving Debtor. A servant of the king owes the king an enormous amount of money. When it is time to repay his debt, he goes before the king and begs for the king's mercy and asks for more time to repay his debt. His request is granted. Later, this same debtor faces a fellow servant whom he has loaned money to. The other servant reacts the same way he did when the time came to repay; he requests more time. However, the first servant does not have mercy on his fellow servant like the king had for him. Instead, he requests his money right away. The king got wind of this and took retribution on the first servant because the servant failed to extend grace to his fellow servant. Jesus warns that if we do not forgive others of their debts, then our heavenly father will not forgive us.

From this example of the unforgiving debtor, we see that we can actually cut our blessings short by not extending forgiveness and grace to others. We have to determine what is most important- money dispensed to assist others or our relationship with Christ. The choice is ours. Hopefully, we will make the right choice.

In Matthew chapter twenty verses 1-18, Jesus shares the parable of the Vineyard Workers. In this story, a landowner went out to hire day laborers to work in his vineyard. Later in the evening, the owner once again went to the market place and hired more day laborers. At the end of the work day, the landowner told the foreman to pay the workers. The foreman did as he was told. He paid all the workers beginning with the last to be hired. Each worker that was hired in the latter part of the day received a full day's pay. At the sight of this, those who were hired in the morning assumed that they would be paid more because they had worked longer hours. To their dismay, they too received the same pay as those who were hired in the evening- a day's earning. With this, they were displeased.

The landowner overheard and addressed their concerns by asking them if they had agreed to work for a day's earnings. He told them to take their earnings and to leave, for they had not been cheated. They had received no less than what they had expected in the beginning to receive. His reasoning, as the one who was dispensing the pay, was that it was up to him as to whether or not he wanted to pay the other laborers more than they actually earned. Since it was his money, he had every right to do so. Jesus says at the end of the parable that the last will be first and the first will be last. God's favor is not dispensed based on the calculations of man. What we may see as fair is based on our human condition, but God weighs things in the spirit. We should be careful to do the same. We should be careful about judging others about who they decide to help. It is neither our responsibility nor our business to decide who should be granted favors or special treatment. This type of judgment leads to jealousy and bitterness, which can interrupt our own blessings. It is best to leave the decision making about blessings to the one who does the blessing.

In Matthew chapter twenty-five verses 14-28, Jesus tells the disciples the parable of the Loaned Money, also known as the parable of the Talents. A man, who was going on a long journey, gave three of his servants some of his money, in proportion to their abilities. To one servant he gave one talent, to another he gave two talents, and to the third he gave five talents. The servants who were given the two and five talents put the money to work for them in an effort to gain more. They were both successful. The one with two talents doubled his money as did the one with five. The servant who was given but one talent decided to place his money in a hole in the ground so that he would not lose his master's money. He did not want to receive harsh treatment from a master he considered to be ruthless.

When the master returned and heard all three accounts from the servants, he rejoiced when he heard of the money earned by the two, but he was outraged when he heard about the servant who was given one talent. As a result, the one talent was taken away from the senseless servant and given to the servant who originally had five talents. This very act is indicative of what God will do to us if we do not wisely use the talents He has blessed us with. God has given us the power to get wealth (Deut. 8:17). For many of us, the power sits in the palm of our hands, yet we fail to tap into it. Instead, we leave our talents buried and we wait for others to bless us when we could be a blessing to others.

However, there are always some who choose to do just the opposite. Let us go to the book of John. In the second chapter verses 13-16, we can see an example of people who have talents but their exercising of them is misplaced. Here, we find Jesus in the temple chasing out merchants who are defiling the house of the Lord. Their business transactions are getting in the way of worship. God wants us to exercise our God-given talents, but worshipping and praising Him comes first. He will not be disrespected or nor will He be put in second place. Let this story be a lesson for us. We are to use our talents wisely and we should bring glory and honor to God in the process.

With each of these parables, we have surveyed several cases about money, gifts, and talents and the blessings and the mismanagement that may result. But we must realize that monetary gifts are not always what a person needs. Sometimes a person just needs favor in his/her life. Look at the story in Acts 3:1-6. Each day, a lame man was brought inside the temple gates called Beautiful so that he could pan handle. One day, Peter and John came into the temple and the man asked them for money. Peter cut short his expectations by telling him that he did not have any silver or gold to give to him, but he could give him what he had. At that point, he told him to get up and walk in the name of Jesus Christ of Nazareth. Peter took the man by the hand and helped him up. In the process, the man was healed instantly. He began walking, leaping, and praising God. This is exactly what we should do when we experience the goodness of the Lord. Also, we have to be careful not to take our blessings for granted which at times we tend to do. We should daily thank the Father for His provisions.

The following story illustrates a person who was blessed with riches here on earth, but because of his earthly conduct with his riches, he did not gain heavenly riches. Instead, he was sentenced to a life in torment. In the book of Luke, in the sixteenth chapter verses 19-31, a rich man failed to share his riches with the poor and downtrodden, namely a poor man named Lazarus. After Lazarus' death, he was taken to be with the forefather Abraham. After the rich man's death, his soul was taken to the place of the dead. While being tormented, he could see Lazarus in the distance. At that point, He begged for mercy and for Lazarus to come and dip the tip of his finger in water to cool his tongue. Even in his present condition, the man still acted as if though he was superior and should be granted favors. Obviously, he had not learned his lesson. Simply put, our actions on this earth will determine God's actions toward us. If we love our neighbors and treat them justly and fairly, we can expect as much from the king. If we do not, we should not expect good in return.

From these lessons, we can see that it may not be monetary gifts that come to bless us, but other gifts which come in all shapes and sizes to help us in a variety of ways. We must also realize that all gifts are from God and are not dispensed evenly amongst men; rather, they are given by God's unmerited favor to whom God himself sees fit. He knows who can handle the gifts and exactly what we will do with them, and if by some chance we choose to misuse our gifts, we can expect to be dealt with accordingly like the rich man in the above story.

Utter a word of prayer for finances, talents, and gifts of kindness.

Father,

In the name of my Lord and Savior, Jesus Christ, I come in your presence thanking you for the many blessing that you have bestowed upon me. Thank you first for the gift of life that you breathe into me daily. Thank for the food and shelter that you have graced me with. Thank you for my loved ones who serve as companions as we walk through this narrow way. Lord, thank you for being my all-in-all. Thank you for always making a way out of no way. Thank you for doing what I could not do. Thank you for always having a ram in the bush for me. Father, thank you for being Jehovah Jirah- my provider and Jehovah Shalom- my peace. Thank you, Lord, for everything. And Father, I pray that you will continue to bless me with the things I need in this life.

In Jesus' name,

Amen.

Scriptures on Finances

3 John 2 *Beloved, I wish above all things that thou mayest prosper and be in health, even as thy soul prospereth.*

Psalm 37:25 *I have been young, and now am old; yet have I not seen the righteous forsaken, nor his seed begging bread.*

Psalm 34:10 *The young lions do lack, and suffer hunger: but they that seek the Lord shall not want any good thing.*

Psalm 23:1 *The Lord is my shepherd; I shall not want.*

Deuteronomy 28:2-8 *And all these blessings shall come on thee, and overtake thee, if thou shalt hearken unto the voice of the Lord thy God. Blessed shalt thou be in the city, and blessed shalt thou be in the field. Blessed shall be the fruit of thy body, and the fruit of thy ground, and the fruit of thy cattle, the increase of thy kine, and the flocks of thy sheep. Blessed shall be thy basket and thy store. Blessed shalt thou be when thou comest in, and blessed shalt thou be when thou goest out. The Lord shall cause thine enemies that rise up against thee to be smitten before thy face: they shall come out against thee one way, and flee before thee seven ways. The Lord shall command the blessing upon thee in thy storehouses, and in all that thou settest thine hand unto; and he shall bless thee in the land which the Lord thy God giveth thee.*

Deuteronomy 28:11-13 *And the Lord shall make thee plenteous in goods, in the fruit of thy body, and in the fruit of thy cattle, and in the fruit of thy ground, in the land which the Lord sware unto thy fathers to give thee. The Lord shall open unto thee his good treasure, the heaven to give the rain unto thy land in his season, and to bless all the work of thine hand: and thou shalt lend unto many nations, and thou shalt not borrow. And the Lord shall make thee the head, and not the tail; and thou shalt be above only, and thou shalt not be beneath; if that thou hearken unto the commandments of the Lord thy God, which I command thee this day, to observe and to do them.*

Deuteronomy 8:7-14 *For the Lord thy God bringeth thee into a good land, a land of brooks of water, of fountains and depths that spring out of valleys and hills; A land of wheat, and barley, and vines, and fig trees, and pomegranates; a land of oil olive, and honey; A land herein thou shalt eat bread without scarceness, thou shalt not lack any thing in it; a land whose stones are iron, and out of whose hills thou mayest dig brass. When thou hast eaten and art full, then thou shalt bless the Lord thy God for the good land which he hath given thee. Beware that thou forget not the Lord thy God, in not keeping his commandments, and his judgments, and his statutes, which I command thee this day: Lest when thou hast eaten and art full, and hast built goodly houses, and dwelt therein; And when thy herds and thy flocks multiply, and thy silver and thy gold is multiplied, and all that thou hast is multiplied; Then thine heart be lifted up, and thou forget the Lord thy God, which brought thee forth out of the land of Egypt, from the house of bondage.*

Luke 6:38 *Give, and it shall be given unto you; good measure, pressed down, and shaken together, and running over, shall men give into your bosom. For with the same measure that ye mete withal it shall be measured to you again.*

I Corinthians 16:2 *Upon the first day of the week let every one of you lay by him in store, as God hath prospered him, that there be no gatherings when I come.*

Matthew 6:31-33 *Therefore take no thought, saying, What shall we eat? or, What shall we drink? or, Wherewithal shall we be clothed? (For after all these things do the Gentiles seek:) for your heavenly Father knoweth that ye have need of all these things. But seek ye first the kingdom of God, and his righteousness; and all these things shall be added unto you.*

Malachi 3:10-12 *Bring ye all the tithes into the storehouse, that there may be meat in mine house, and prove me now herewith, saith the Lord of hosts, if I will not open you the windows of heaven, and pour you out a blessing, that there shall not be room enough to receive it. And I will rebuke the devourer for your sakes, and he shall not destroy the fruits of your ground; neither shall your vine cast her fruit before the time in the field, saith the Lord of hosts. And all nations shall call you blessed: for ye shall be a delightsome land, saith the Lord of hosts.*

Joshua 1:8 *This book of the law shall not depart out of thy mouth; but thou shalt meditate therein day and night, that thou mayest observe to do according to all that is written therein: for then thou shalt make thy way prosperous, and then thou shalt have good success.*

Proverbs 13:22 *A good man leaveth an inheritance to his children's children: and the wealth of the sinner is laid up for the just.*

Philippians 4:19 *But my God shall supply all your need according to his riches in glory by Christ Jesus.*

2 Corinthians 9:6-8 *But this I say, He which soweth sparingly shall reap also sparingly; and he which soweth bountifully shall reap also bountifully. Every man according as he purposeth in his heart, so let him give; not grudgingly, or of necessity: for God loveth a cheerful giver. And God is able to make all grace abound toward you; that ye, always having all sufficiency in all things, may abound to every good work.*

Glimmers of Hope

56

Through the Storm   C. White-Elliott

Be Encouraged

A young man had been to Wednesday Night Bible Study. The pastor had shared about listening to God and obeying the Lord's voice. The young man couldn't help but wonder, "Does God still speak to people?" After service, he went out with some friends for coffee and pie and they discussed the message. Several different ones talked about how God had led them in different ways. It was about ten o'clock when the young man started driving home. Sitting in his car, he just began to pray, "God...If you still speak to people, speak to me. I will listen. I will do my best to obey."

As he drove down the main street of his town, he had the strangest thought to stop and buy a gallon of milk. He shook his head and said out loud, "God is that you?" He didn't get a reply and started on toward home. But again, the thought, buy a gallon of milk came into his head. The young man thought about Samuel and how he didn't recognize the voice of God, and how little Samuel ran to Eli. "Okay, God, in case that is you, I will buy the milk." It didn't seem like too hard a test of obedience. He could always use the milk. He stopped and purchased the gallon of milk and started off toward home.

As he passed Seventh Street, he again felt the urge, "Turn down that street." This is crazy he thought and drove on past the intersection. Again, he felt that he should turn down Seventh Street. At the next intersection, he turned back and headed down Seventh.

Half jokingly, he said out loud, "Okay, God. I will." He drove several blocks, when suddenly, he felt like he should stop. He pulled

87

over to the curb and looked around. He was in a semi-commercial area of town. It wasn't the best but it wasn't the worst of neighborhoods either. The businesses were closed and most of the houses looked dark like the people were already in bed. Again, he sensed something, "Go and give the milk to the people in the house across the street." The young man looked at the house. It was dark and it looked like the people were either gone or they were already asleep. He started to open the door and then sat back in the car seat.

"Lord, this is insane. Those people are asleep and if I wake them up, they are going to be mad and I will look stupid." Again, he felt like he should go and give the milk. Finally, he opened the door, "Okay God, if this is you, I will go to the door and I will give them the milk. If you want me to look like a crazy person, okay. I want to be obedient. I guess that will count for something, but if they don't answer right away, I am out of here."

He walked across the street and rang the bell. He could hear some noise inside. A man's voice yelled out, "Who is it? What do you want?" Then the door opened before the young man could get away. The man was standing there in his jeans and T-shirt. He looked like he just got out of bed. He had a strange look on his face and he didn't seem too happy to have some stranger standing on his doorstep. "What is it?" The young man thrust out the gallon of milk, "Here, I brought this to you." The man took the milk and rushed down a hallway.

Then from down the hall came a woman carrying the milk toward the kitchen. The man was following her holding a baby. The baby was crying. The man had tears streaming down his face. The man began speaking and half crying, "We were just praying. We had some big bills this month and we ran out of money. We didn't have any milk for our baby. I was just praying and asking God to show me how to get some milk." His wife in the kitchen yelled out, "I asked Him to send an angel with some. Are you an angel?" The young man reached into his wallet and pulled out all the money he had on him and put it in the man's hand. He turned and walked back toward his car and the tears were streaming down his face.

He knew that God still answers prayers.

This story has so many lessons imbedded in it. Let's focus on the topic of finances and the favor of God. Here, the man and his wife needed milk for their baby and did not have the money because they had spent the money on other expenses, but they had the favor of God. That is all they needed.

What Goes Around Comes Around

He almost didn't see the old lady, stranded on the side of the road, but even in the dim light of day, he could see she needed help. So he pulled up in front of her Mercedes and got out. His Pontiac was still sputtering when he approached her. Even with the smile on his face, she was worried. No one had stopped to help for the last hour or so.

Was he going to hurt her? He didn't look safe; he looked poor and hungry.

He could see that she was frightened, standing out there in the cold. He knew how she felt. It was that chill that only fear can put in you. He said, "I'm here to help you, ma'am. Why don't you wait in the car where it's warm? By the way, my name is Bryan Anderson."

Well, all she had was a flat tire; but for an old lady, that was bad enough. Bryan crawled under the car looking for a place to put the jack, skinning his knuckles a time or two. Soon he was able to change the tire, but he had to get dirty and his hands hurt. As he was tightening up the lug nuts, she rolled down the window and began to talk to him. She told him that she was from St. Louis and was only just passing through. She couldn't thank him enough for coming to her aid. Bryan just smiled as he closed her trunk. The lady asked how much she owed him. Any amount would have been all right with her. She already imagined all the awful things that could have happened had he not stopped.

Bryan never thought twice about being paid. This was not a job to him. This was helping someone in need, and God knows there were plenty, who had given him a hand in the past. He had lived his whole life that way, and it never occurred to him to act any other way. He told her that if she really wanted to pay him back, the next time she saw someone who needed help, she could give that person the assistance they needed, and Bryan added, "And think of me."

He waited until she started her car and drove off. It had been a cold and depressing day, but he felt good as he headed for home, disappearing into the twilight.

A few miles down the road, the lady saw a small cafe. She went in to grab a bite to eat and take the chill off before she made the last leg of her trip home. It was a dingy looking restaurant. Outside were two old gas pumps.

The whole scene was unfamiliar to her. The waitress came over and brought a clean towel to wipe her wet hair. She had a sweet smile, one that even being on her feet for the whole day couldn't erase. The lady noticed the waitress was nearly eight months pregnant, but she never let the strain and aches change her attitude. The old lady wondered how someone who had so little could be so giving to a stranger. Then she remembered Bryan.

After the lady finished her meal, she paid with a hundred dollar bill. The waitress quickly went to get change for her hundred dollar bill, but the old lady had slipped right out the door. She was gone by the time the waitress came back. The waitress wondered where the lady could be.

Then she noticed something written on the napkin. There were tears in her eyes when she read what the lady wrote: "You don't owe me anything. I have been there too. Somebody once helped me out, the way I'm helping you. If you really want to pay me back, here is what you do: Do not let this chain of love end with you."

Under the napkin were four more $100 bills.

Well, there were tables to clear, sugar bowls to fill, and people to serve, but the waitress made it through another day. That night when she got home from work and climbed into bed, she was thinking about the money and what the lady had written. How could the lady have known how much she and her husband needed it? With the baby due next month, it was going to be hard....

She knew how worried her husband was, and as he lay sleeping next to her, she gave him a soft kiss and whispered soft and low, "Everything's going to be all right. I love you, Bryan Anderson." There is an old saying, "What goes around comes around."

The Letter

Ruth went to her mail box and there was only one letter. She picked it up and looked at it before opening, but then she looked at the envelope again. There was no stamp, no postmark, only her name and address. She read the letter:

Dear Ruth:

I'm going to be in your neighborhood Saturday afternoon and I'd like to stop by for a visit.

Love Always,

Jesus

Her hands were shaking as she placed the letter on the table. "Why would the Lord want to visit me? I'm nobody special. I don't have anything to offer."

With that thought, Ruth remembered her empty kitchen cabinets. "Oh my goodness, I really don't have anything to offer. I'll have to run down to the store and buy something for dinner." She reached for her purse and counted out its contents. Five dollars and forty cents. Well, I can get some bread and cold cuts, at least." She threw on her coat and hurried out the door. A loaf of French bread, a half-pound of sliced turkey, and a carton of milk....leaving Ruth with grand total twelve cents to last her until Monday. Nonetheless, she felt good as she headed home, her meager offerings tucked under her arm.

"Hey lady, can you help us, lady?" Ruth had been so absorbed in her dinner plans, she hadn't even noticed two figures huddled in the alleyway. A man and a woman, both of them dressed in little more than rags. "Look lady, I ain't got a job, ya know, and my wife and I have been living out here on the street, and, well, now it's getting cold and we're getting kinda hungry and, well, if you could help us. Lady, we'd really appreciate it." Ruth looked at them both. They were dirty, they smelled bad and frankly, she was certain that they could get some kind of work if they really wanted to.

"Sir, I'd like to help you, but I'm a poor woman myself. All I have is a few cold cuts and some bread, and I'm having an important guest for dinner tonight and I was planning on serving that to Him."

"Yeah, well, okay lady, I understand. Thanks anyway." The man put his arm around the woman's shoulders, turned and headed back into the alley. As she watched them leave, Ruth felt a familiar twinge in her heart.

"Sir, wait!"

The couple stopped and turned as she ran down the alley after them.

"Look, why don't you take this food. I'll figure out something else to serve my guest."

She handed the man her grocery bag.

"Thank you lady. Thank you very much!"

"Yes, thank you!" It was the man's wife, and Ruth could see now that she was shivering.

"I have another coat at home. Here, why don't you take this one."

Ruth unbuttoned her jacket and slipped it over the woman's shoulders. Then smiling, she turned and walked back to the street...without her coat and with nothing to serve her guest.

"Thank you, lady! Thank you very much!"

Ruth was chilled by the time she reached her front door and worried too. The Lord was coming to visit and she didn't have anything to offer Him. She fumbled through her purse for the door key. But as she did, she noticed another envelope in her mailbox. "That's odd. The mailman doesn't usually come twice in one day."

Dear Ruth:

It was so good to see you again. Thank you for the lovely meal. And thank you, too, for the beautiful coat.

Love Always,

Jesus

The air was still cold, but even without her coat, Ruth no longer noticed.

The Unemployed Graduate

An unemployed graduate woke up one morning and checked his pocket. All he had left was $10. He decided to use it to buy food and then wait for death as he was too proud to go begging. He was frustrated as he could find no job, and nobody was ready to help him. He bought food and as he sat down to eat, an old man and two little children came along and asked him to help them with food as they had not eaten for almost a week. He looked at them. They were so lean that he could see their bones coming out. Their eyes had gone into the sockets. With the last bit of compassion he had, he gave them the food.

The old man and children prayed that God would bless and prosper him and then gave him a very old coin. The young graduate said to them, "You need the prayer more than I do." With no money, no job, no food, the young graduate went under the bridge to rest and wait for death. As he was about to sleep, he saw an old newspaper on the ground. He picked it up, and suddenly he saw an advertisement for people with old coins to come to a certain address. He decided to go there with the old coin the old man gave him.

On getting to the place, he gave the proprietor the coin. The proprietor screamed, brought out a big book and showed the young graduate a photograph. This same old coin was worth 3 million dollars. The young graduate was overjoyed as the proprietor gave him a bank draft for 3 million dollars within an hour. He collected the bank draft and went in search of the old man and little children. By the time he got to where he left them eating, they had gone. He asked the owner of the canteen if he knew them. He said, "No, but they left a note for you." He quickly opened the note thinking it would lead him to find them. This is what the note said: "You gave us your all and we have rewarded you back with the coin." Signed God the Father, The Son and The Holy Ghost. 1 Kings 17:10-16; Matthew 11:28-30.

Have you given all to Jesus Christ? If you haven't, do so today and he will surprise you.

Four

Who Am I?

Let me begin this chapter by asking you a question in the form of a poem that I wrote several years ago.

<u>Who Are You?</u>

When people see you, what do you want them to see?
What should the determinants be?

Do you want them to determine who you are
By characteristics such as gender, race, and creed, or something more meaningful
  by far?

Although these characteristics are part of you,
They don't define your self-worth or the things you do.

How do you feel when people think you fit a specific stereotype?
What are their assumptions based on, a scientific prototype?

What you have done and have potential to do
Should be the important things that speak for you.

Don't let the world's prejudices bring you down.
Wear a smile on your face instead of a frown.

Work hard to achieve your goals as you experience life.
And don't let others make you sacrifice.

Or give up your dreams, your self-esteem, or your hopes.
Stand tall and proud and remember to cope.

With a world full of prejudices and regrets,
Remember who you are in spite of it.

In this poem, I identify several attributes that the enemy tries to use to define and limit who we are: race, gender, creed, prejudices, and stereotypes. Many times we fall victim to the snares that the enemy sets for us through the words of other people. We listen intently to what they say about us. If they offer positive affirmations, we feel wonderful. If they offer obscenities about us, we are hurt. The degree to how wonderful we feel or how bad we feel depends on how we view ourselves. If we feel confident about whom God made us, when we receive positive comments we will take them in stride. The comments will not cause us to become lifted up in pride. Although the accolades will be appreciated, the comments will come to confirm and re-affirm what God already told us about ourselves. If, on the other hand, we doubt our abilities and struggle with our self concepts, the positive comments can be an open door for the spirit of pride to come in, as we will not be able to handle them.

The same effect is true with negative, offensive comments. The comments come as stinging darts, which are often times fiery. If we have a healthy self esteem, we will see the comments for what they are. They come to make us question who we are in Christ and the abilities/talents He gave us. However, if our self esteem is low, the fiery darts can have a devastating effect on us, which can be long lasting.

The key to our responses is knowing exactly who we are in Christ. Romans 12:3 states, *"For I say, through the grace given unto me, to every man that is among you, not to think of himself more highly than he ought to think; but to think soberly, according as God hath dealt to every man the measure of faith."* We are uniquely designed. The only one who can give us an accurate account of who we are is our creator. Only the one who creates knows the purpose for the creation. Therefore, rather than searching for your self worth through the comments of man, ask God, as He is our creator. If you consider God to be your source for your health, your finances, for forgiveness, for peace, for joy, etcetera, then consider Him as your source to tell you your purpose for being on earth.

Some of our most perilous times of questioning ourselves are when we are in the midst of a storm. When we are going through trials and dealing with the curve balls that life throws us, we should just focus on the problem at hand. This is not the time to focus on whether or not we are doing what God called us to do. Read the following scenario.

A minister recently launched out into ministry by opening his own church, after hearing the voice of the Lord. During the first few years, many people joined the church; some remained and others left. He even faced financial troubles as he attempted to get the church off the ground. Some weeks the tithes and offerings paid the bills; other weeks they did not. He suffered attacks from the congregation, as they began to witness the struggles the church was having and question his calling. However, while he suffered these adverse attacks, he still kept his joy, even in the midnight hour. He still had members who loved him and would stay with him for life. They continued to bring new converts and sheep to the church. He was determined to not get discouraged.

But then, on one gloomy day, he arrived at the church for Morning Prayer and there was a yellow note attached to the door. There was also a padlock on the door preventing him from entering the house of God. He was totally devastated by the recent occurrence of events. He left the church and went home. No one heard from him for a week. The members all saw the note on the door, for some had come for Morning Prayer and others had come for mid-week bible study. The members did not know what to do. They tried calling the pastor but to no avail. The pastor was not taking any calls.

While he was home, he cried out to the Lord. During his prayers, he asked for clarity. As he opened his bible, he asked for a rhema word. But unfortunately, he heard nothing. Finally, he began to conclude that maybe he had not heard the voice of the Lord. Maybe he was just on a journey and was not following God's direction. All he could think of were all the downfalls he had suffered after he opened the church.

He did not think of all the lives that were changed. He did not remember the little girl he prayed for when doctors told her mother that the little girl's leg needed to be amputated but in the end it did not. He did not remember the family who lost their home and took shelter in the church. He did not remember the thousands of families the church fed week after week with the food program. He did not remember how God used him in a mighty way against the war on drugs and the gang activities in the community where the church was situated. He did not remember.

As the days and nights wore on, the pastor furiously paced the floor feeling dismayed and distraught. He did not know how he could face his congregation and tell them that the work he had started in the name of the Lord was not ordained by the Lord. He felt that if it was ordained by God then he would not have failed. Finally, after about a week, he mustered up the courage to speak to his members. He contacted his secretary and asked her to call the members to come for a meeting at a neighborhood restaurant that was just down the street from the church. He planned to tell them that he would no longer be their pastor and that he was sorry for any undue hardship that the dissolving of the church would place on their families.

As he drove over to the restaurant, he had to pass the church on the way. It hurt his heart to lift his head in the direction of the church because he felt like a failure that had let himself, his members and the community down. Most importantly, he felt like he let God down. He believed that he was not living up to his true calling. As he lifted his eyes to view the church that he so lovingly came to day after day for over three years, his eyes met features on the church that were unfamiliar to him. His first thought was that the city had already leased the building out to someone else because of his failure to pay or contact them. But as he gazed closer at the new marquee that was placed just to the right of the church, he noticed that it displayed the church name in lights- A Place of New Beginnings Deliverance Church. He did not understand what was going on, so he pulled into the church parking lot to find out. As he walked around to the front door, he noticed that the hideous yellow note was no longer attached to it and the padlock had been removed.

He reached down to turn the knob so that he could enter the building, but someone opened it from the inside. It was Big George, one of the ex-gang members from the community.

"Pastor, hey. How's it going?"

"Um, George, what are you doing here? What's going on?"

"You know, Pastor, me and some of the fellas saw the note on the door and we have been trying to call you all week. Ms. Ella didn't know what to do 'cause she hadn't heard from you. Finally, she called the city and they told her what was going on with the building. Me and the fellas got some money together and took care of the problem."

"Wow. I don't know…"

"Awe, Pastor. You don't have to say anything. It was the least we could do."

"Thank you, George. Please tell the others that I said thank you also. I don't know how I can repay you or when."

"No, we are not asking that you repay us. We wanted to do it. You have done so much for this community. Most of us were raised Catholic, but your church has done so much for us and our community. You have actually taught us something about self respect and respecting others. We used to do stupid stuff, but we try to help out more. Oh, and the guys are inside."

Once the pastor and Big George went inside, the pastor talked to some of the other ex-gang members and other members of the community. They had banded together to save the church. All the pastor could do was cry. He knelt before the altar and repented for not holding steadfast to his faith. He had thought that God would move through the members of the congregation. But God had his own plan in mind.

As the pastor knelt at the altar, he began to remember all the good that the building of the church made in the community and in the lives of the community members. He remembered watching the little girl learn how to jump rope. Something she would not have done if her leg would have been amputated. He remembered how the church banded together to find a home for a displaced family. He remembered the substance abuse treatment programs that the church sponsored, and how so many lives were turned around. He remembered the home for abused women that the women's department volunteered in. At the altar, he remembered all that the Holy Spirit had done through the church.

Many of us find ourselves in similar situations that cause us to question who we are and if we are doing God's will for our lives. In doing so, we also tend to limit God with our expectations, instead of moving out of God's way so that He can move as He chooses. Does that mean that we really limit God? No. It means that we limit the boundaries of our faith. We limit what we believe about ourselves and even about God, sometimes due to words uttered by other people. We can never limit God, just as in the case of the pastor. The pastor's faith was limited, which was caused greatly by what some of his parishioners said. But God worked out the situation the way He saw fit, whether or not the pastor believed that it would be done. That was just another lesson for the pastor. And we too can learn from this lesson.

During his time of trial, the pastor took his eyes off God and began to look at the situation. While looking at the situation, he began to question himself, after some of the flock questioned him and his calling. As stated earlier in this chapter, when we go through trials, we need to focus on the trial at hand. It is not the time to question our existence. We may need to question it afterwards, but at the time of the trial we need to focus on the problem at hand and seek God for directions to solve the problem. The pastor could have continued to wait for the manifestation of God's blessing while praying and fasting and going about his daily activities, he could have continued to pastor the flock that God had given him, and he could have called the city to reach an agreement with them regarding his lease. Instead, he focused on whether or not he was in God's will and he did nothing.

Even if he was not in God's will, did that relinquish him from the responsibilities that he had created? No, it did not. Therefore, he still had obligations that he had to fulfill. The devil is very crafty about getting us to shift our focus; he will slither in at a moment's notice to throw us off course. We have to keep a watchful eye and be aware of his devices. The bible says that, *"Lest Satan should get an advantage of us: for we are not ignorant of his devices"* (2 Corinthians 2:11).

In situations like these, we must continue to stand on the word that we daily confess. We cannot waiver. The word tells us, *"that we henceforth be no more children tossed to and fro and carried about with every word of doctrine by the sleight of men, and cunning craftiness, whereby they lie in wait to deceive"* (Ephesians 4:14). The pastor, like many of us, let our immediate circumstances and the word of others carry us away from God's word and the inherent promises. It is much more beneficial and time effective if we stay with the truth- the word of God.

To do this, we just need to follow the instructions that are given in Ephesians. Chapter six verses 11-13 tell us how to be fully equipped to withstand trials and tests. It says we are to, *"Put on the whole armour of God, that ye may be able to stand against the wiles of the devil. For we wrestle not against flesh and blood, but against principalities, against powers, against the rulers of the darkness of this world, against spiritual wickedness in high places. Wherefore take unto you the whole armour of God, that ye may be able to withstand in the evil day, and having done all, to stand. Stand therefore, having your loins girt about with truth, and having on the breastplate of righteousness."*

Being fully protected and equipped for battle does not cause us to be exempt from the fiery darts of the enemy, but it will enable us to stand firm and to be more than a conqueror when the enemy rears his ugly head in our direction trying to find a hole in our armour. Let's pray.

Father God,

I thank you that I know who I am in you. I thank you that I do not have to question my identity or my purpose. I am a child of the Most High god, who reigns supreme. I am a peculiar person that was created to serve the King of Kings. I am unique in my design, for there is no other person like me on the face of this earth. I have abilities and talents that were part of my make up before I departed from my mother's womb. I am special to you Lord because you made me. I pray that you will continue to sharpen me Lord and continue to equip me for your service. I pray also that as I go through this life that I will be an example to others and let my light shine. Thank you Lord for setting me apart and using me for your glory. Thank you for allowing me to see clearly and for not letting the enemy play tricks with my mind in an effort to deceive me. Thank you for the tests and the trials that come that are designed to make me stronger. Thank you allowing me to walk in the authority that you gave me and with the confidence to know who I am. I thank you, Lord. And I bless your name. I give you praise, honor, and glory for turning my doubting mind around, and I shall never revisit this doubting stage again.

In Jesus' name,

Amen.

How can I help someone I love?

Do you know someone who is struggling with who he/she is and what his/her role is here on earth? What has God shown you about this individual? Now is the time for you to speak life into his/her situation. Tell him/her exactly what God has told you and let him/her know that this is what God says. Then after telling him/her what God says, tell him/her what you yourself have witnessed about his/her abilities, character, and integrity. Discuss with the individual the strengths that he/she possesses. Encourage the person with everything you have within you. What do you have to lose? Nothing. But you have everything to gain and so does the other person. Once the person catches on to whom God has created him/her to be, both of you will rejoice.

Pray the following prayer.

Dear Lord,

I come before you thanking you that I know who I am in you. Thank you for creating me to be unique. Father, I come to you today on behalf of _____, whom you also uniquely designed, as you have made all your creations. Lord, you have gifted <u>her or him,</u> with the ability to _____. I thank you Lord for <u>his or her</u> talents and I pray that you will remind <u>her or him</u> that <u>he or she</u> is your child and that you made <u>him or her</u> part of the royal priesthood along with all your other heirs. Father, show me how I can be of assistance in revealing my friend's true personhood. I am willing and available to be used of you, Father. I am ready to do your will. My friend is important to the building of your kingdom, and I do not want <u>him or her</u> to fall by the wayside. Oh miracle-working God, show <u>him or her</u> a sign to let <u>him or her</u> know that you have not forsaken <u>him or her.</u>

In the mighty name of Jesus,

Amen.

The following poem really captured my attention and pierced my heart when one of my students who wrote it shared it with me.

Who Is This Woman?

Who is this woman, whose life has become

One long journey, and a ridged one.

Who is this woman, you look at and see

Her sorrow and pain and a heart that grieves

Who is this woman, who has lost her way

Whose nights are so dark, she can't see the day

Who is this woman, whose heart is so hardened she's unable to cry

She wears the mask of deception and lies

The hurt and the anger that has made her bare

A deep longing loss, she's unable to share

Yet, she still carries on … as if she doesn't care

Who is this woman I see, but do not like?

Who struggles for peace with all her might

Who is this woman, I so blatantly see?

When I look in the mirror

    The woman is ME!!!!!!!!

La'Shelle Topps

Scriptures on Self Concepts

Romans 12:3 "*For I say, through the grace given unto me, to every man that is among you, not to think of himself more highly than he ought to think; but to think soberly, according as God hath dealt to every man the measure of faith.*"

2 Timothy 1:7 *For God hath not given us the spirit of fear; but of power, and of love, and of a sound mind.*

James 1:5 *If any of you lack wisdom, let him ask of God, that giveth to all men liberally, and upbraideth not; and it shall be given him.*

Proverbs 3:5-6 *Trust in the Lord with all thine heart; and lean not unto thine own understanding. In all thy ways acknowledge him, and he shall direct thy paths.*

Psalm 32:8 *I will instruct thee and teach thee in the way which thou shalt go: I will guide thee with mine eye.*

1 Peter 4:12-13 *Beloved, think it not strange concerning the fiery trial which is to try you, as though some strange thing happened unto you: But rejoice, inasmuch as ye are partakers of Christ's sufferings; that, when his glory shall be revealed, ye may be glad also with exceeding joy.*

Isaiah 43:2 *When thou passest through the waters, I will be with thee; and through the rivers, they shall not overflow thee: when thou walkest through the fire, thou shalt not be burned; neither shall the flame kindle upon thee.*

Philippians 4:6-7 *Be careful for nothing; but in every thing by prayer and supplication with thanksgiving let your requests be made known unto God. And the peace of God, which passeth all understanding, shall keep your hearts and minds through Christ Jesus.*

Glimmers of Hope

The Duck & the Devil

There was a little boy visiting his grandparents on their farm. He was given a slingshot to play with out in the woods. He practiced in the woods; but he could never hit the target. Getting a little discouraged, he headed back for dinner.

As he was walking back he saw Grandma's pet duck. Just out of impulse, he let the slingshot fly, hit the duck square in the head and killed it. He was shocked and grieved! In a panic, he hid the dead duck in the wood pile, only to see his sister watching! Sally had seen it all, but she said nothing. After lunch the next day, Grandma said, "Sally, let's wash the dishes." But Sally said, "Grandma, Johnny told me he wanted to help in the kitchen." Then she whispered to him, "Remember the duck?" So, Johnny did the dishes. Later that day, Grandpa asked if the children wanted to go fishing and Grandma said, "I'm sorry but I need Sally to help make supper."

Sally just smiled and said, "Well that's all right because Johnny told me he wanted to help." She whispered again, "Remember the duck?" So Sally went fishing and Johnny stayed to help. After several days of Johnny doing both his chores and Sally's, he finally couldn't stand it any longer. He came to Grandma and confessed that he had killed the duck. Grandma knelt down, gave him a hug and said, "Sweetheart, I know. You see, I was standing at the window and I saw the whole thing, but because I love you, I forgave you. I was just wondering how long you would let Sally make a slave of you." Thought for the day and every day thereafter: whatever is in your past, whatever you have done... and the devil keeps throwing it up in your face (lying, cheating, debt, fear, bad habits, hatred, anger, bitterness, etc.)...whatever it is...You need to know that God was standing at the window and He saw the whole thing. He has seen your whole life. He wants you to know that He loves you and that you are forgiven.

He's just wondering how long you will let the devil make a slave of you. The great thing about God is that when you ask for forgiveness, He not only forgives you, but He forgets. It is by God's grace and mercy that we are saved.

The Real Me

Malachi 3:3 says: "He will sit as a refiner and purifier of silver."

This verse puzzled some women in a bible study and they wondered what this statement meant about the character and nature of God. One of the women offered to find out the process of refining silver and get back to the group at their next bible Study.

That week, the woman called a silversmith and made an appointment to watch him at work. She didn't mention anything about the reason for her interest beyond her curiosity about the process of refining silver. As she watched the silversmith, he held a piece of silver over the fire and let it heat up. He explained that in refining silver, one needed to hold the silver in the middle of the fire where the flames were hottest, as to burn away all the impurities.

The woman thought about God holding us in such a hot spot; then she thought again about the verse that says: "He sits as a refiner and purifier of silver." She asked the silversmith if it was true that he had to sit there in front of the fire the whole time the silver was being refined. The man answered that yes, he not only had to sit there holding the silver, but he had to keep his eyes on the silver the entire time it was in the fire. If the silver was left a moment too long in the flames, it would be destroyed.

The woman was silent for a moment. Then she asked the silversmith, "How do you know when the silver is fully refined?" He smiled at her and answered, "Oh, that's easy -- when I see my image in it."

If today you are feeling the heat of the fire, remember that God has his eye on you and will keep watching you until He sees His image in you.

God's Coffee

A group of alumni, highly established in their careers, got to talking at a reunion and decided to go visit their old university professor, now retired. During their visit, the conversation soon turned into complaints about stress in their work and lives. Offering his guests coffee, the professor went to the kitchen and returned with a large pot of coffee and an assortment of cups - porcelain, plastic, glass, crystal, some plain looking, some expensive, some exquisite - telling them to help themselves to the coffee. When all the alumni had a cup of coffee in hand, the professor said, "Notice that all the nice looking, expensive cups were taken up, leaving behind the plain and cheap ones."

While it is normal for you to want only the best for yourselves, that is the source of your problems and stress. Be assured that the cup itself adds no quality to the coffee. In most cases, it is just more expensive and in some cases even hides that we drink.

What all of you really wanted was coffee, not the cup, but you consciously went for the best cups... and then you began eyeing each other's cups. Now consider this: Life is the coffee; your job, money and position in society are the cups. They are just tools to hold and contain Life. The type of cup one has does not define, nor change the quality of life a person lives. Sometimes, by concentrating only on the cup, we fail to enjoy the coffee God has provided us. The happiest people don't have the best of everything. They just make the best of everything." God brews the coffee, not the cups...

Enjoy your coffee!

Live simply.

Love generously.

Care deeply.

Speak kindly.

Spend time with God over your coffee.

 Remember to treasure the life that God gives you. The trimming is just the icing on the cake.

Five

Broken Relationships

"Well, I guess this is for the best."

"I did all I could do."

"I must press on and continue toward the mark and not let this debilitate me."

These are some of the things that I said to myself as my impending divorce came near and was finalized. I did not talk to anyone about my divorce because I did not want to go into details about the sorted mess that I had entangled myself with, nor did I want people to hear the pain and disappointment in my voice. However, what I was actually feeling inside was becoming more and more suppressed from not opening up and talking about it. I thought that not talking about it would help with my desire of wanting it all to be a distant memory. I was soon to find out that the memory was not too far behind me as the pressure of disappointment only seemed to build. My daily existence still questioned why this had happened. It seemed as if more time was needed to heal my wounds.

I found that the reason for my suppressed emotions was that I was not being honest with myself. The reality was my heart was broken into a million pieces, and I was very disappointed. I had failed. I had waited nine years after being divorced from my sons' father to remarry. I had said that the next time I got married would be it for me. I thought it was a match made in heaven. My new husband and I had both been called into ministry and a promising future lay in wait for us. Well, at least that is what I thought. That was only partly true. The other part of our lives was filled with pain, torment and despair. We found ourselves caught in a whirlwind, facing the thin line between love and hate.

Where did we go wrong? How could we not overcome the challenges we were faced with? How could this happen to two children of the Most High God who loved Him dearly and each other? Day and night, I tortured myself with this question.

What I came to realize, though, was that my situation was not at all uncommon. Unfortunately, broken relationships exist everywhere, in small towns and in large cities, in poor communities and with the rich and famous, with the educated and the uneducated. I even found broken relationships in the bible, some that were restored and others that were not. In the book of Esther, for example, the marriage between King Xerxes and Queen Vashti suffered from irreconcilable differences. As a result, in the blink of an eye, their relationship was severed. King Xerxes was giving a banquet and he requested the presence of his wife so that he could display her beauty to all of his guests. Queen Vashti was giving a banquet of her own for the women and therefore refused to grant her husband's request. After conferring with his council, King Xerxes decided that it was best for the other women to not have an example like Queen Vashti in their midst as it may cause further disobedience from wives towards their husbands. Consequently, Queen Vashti was deposed and, eventually, replaced with Queen Esther.

The story of Adam and Eve is also one of a broken relationship. In Genesis Chapter three Verse six, we read that Adam and Eve decided to eat of the tree of Knowledge of Good and Evil, even though it was forbidden. When they broke God's Commandment, they broke a covenant relationship with Him. Their punishment was death, as they were forewarned, in Genesis 2:17, *"But the tree of the knowledge of good and evil, thou shalt not eat of it: for in the day that thou eatest thereof thou shalt surely die."*

Later, after Eve began to bear children, the issue of broken relationships continues. The first born children of Adam and Eve are Cain and Abel. Cain was a farmer; while Abel was a shepherd. When time came to offer a gift to the Lord, both sons offered gifts, but Abel's gift was accepted whereas Cain's gift was not. This hurt Cain terribly and jealousy of his brother set in. Eventually, Cain came up with a plot. One day, he suggested to his brother that they go out into the fields, so they did. While there, Cain slew his younger brother Abel (Genesis 4:3-8). As a result, not only did Cain cause his father and mother to lose one son, eventually they lost two because Cain had to go away to another land, the land of Nod, east of Eden. In Cain's story alone, we see many broken relationships: between brothers, between parents and children, and between God and Cain.

As the book of Genesis continues, we can read about Noah and his three sons: Shem, Ham, and Japeth, in chapters six through ten. After the great flood, Noah and his family returned to dry land and Noah planted a vineyard. One day after drinking some wine that he had made, Noah became intoxicated and lay naked inside his tent. His youngest son Ham witnessed his father's condition and told his two older brothers. His brothers discretely covered their father's condition without witnessing it themselves. When Noah learned of this incident, he was furious. As a result, he cursed Canaan, his grandson, the son of Ham and blessed the descendents of his other two sons.

Still in Genesis, which seems to be overwrought with broken relationships, we find still another one in chapter 16 verses 4-6. In the previous chapter, Abram, a servant of God, was promised a son when he was in his mid-eighties. As his wife Sarai was barren, she decided to offer her husband her servant Hagar so Hagar could bear him a son. Once Hagar became pregnant, she began to treat Sarai with contempt because she knew that she was bearing a child for a man who had none because his wife was barren. After complaining to Abram, Sarai began to treat Hagar harshly and as a result, Hagar fled. However, an angel of the Lord intervened and promptly had a conversation with Hagar showing her the error of her ways. She returned home and bore a son whom she named Ishmael. After this, the relationship between Sarai and Hagar was permanently severed after Isaac was born, which resulted in the severing of a relationship between brothers and father and son.

In the book of Numbers, As Moses is diligently leading the Israelites to the Promised Land, Miriam and Aaron oppose Moses by saying that the Lord speaks to them also. This angered God and He came down in a pillar of cloud and spoke directly to them and asked how they could not be afraid to criticize God's chosen vessel. Upon God's departure, Miriam was left with leprosy. Aaron, in a state of horror and remorse, begged for Moses to not allow them to be punished. Moses cried out on Miriam's behalf. But the Lord saw fit for her to stay infected for seven days before He allowed her return to the camp. Rebellion against God's chosen vessel did not go unpunished; however, the relationship was restored to its original state.

In the book of 2 Samuel chapters 13 and 14, Amnon is found to be in love with his half sister Tamar. Instead of going about the respectable course of asking their father for her hand in marriage (as was permissible in those days), he decided to take matters into his own hands. At Amnon's request, King David allowed his daughter Tamar to go to see her supposedly ill brother and prepare food for him. Unbeknownst to both King David and Tamar, Amnon had devised a wicked plan. Once Tamar had arrived and prepared the food, Amnon asked her to come to bed with him. She flatly refused. She was appalled by the idea and questioned both his and her reputation that would result from such actions. Amnon, on the other hand, did not care. At this point, he proceeded to rape her and then threw her out. With his despicable acts, he severed the relationship between himself and his sister and then also himself and his brother Absalom, who later avenged his sister Tamar by having Amnon killed. As a result of killing Amnon, Absalom created a rift between King David and himself. As demonstrated with this account, one act can cause a broken family, as it did with the act of Cain in Genesis.

Now let us take a time travel over to the New Testament, where we see that conditions are no different. People are still behaving in destructive manners and causing relationships to be broken. Let us take, for example, the new found Christian Paul who was converted on the road to Damascus as he was continuing on his way to persecute more Christians. In Acts 15:36-41, Paul, who whose previously known as Saul, had already completed his first missionary journey with Barnabas. During this trip John Mark, Barnabas' cousin, had traveled along with them but had turned back during the midst of the journey. Paul found this disturbing. When Paul and Barnabas were preparing for a second missionary trip, Barnabas wanted to once again bring John Mark along. Paul flatly refused. He was not interested in a repeat act of the first journey. At his disapproval, the team of Paul and Barnabas split because they could not find a middle ground of compromise. Unlike some of the other accounts where jealousy and murder caused the rifts between families, here we have a case of a disagreement causing the rift.

All throughout the bible, we can find broken relationships between people. However, several times humans suffered from broken relationships with God. In the book of Exodus, the Israelites stray from God and cause themselves to be separated from Him. As time went on and after so much destruction from human sin and separation from God, God himself had to come to earth, in the personhood of his son Jesus Christ, to restore humans back into proper relationship with their creator. It is because of His gift to us that we have been reconnected with the Father and can have a relationship with Him that He intended from the time of our creation.

Now the question to be answered is, "How can we restore a broken relationship with another person?" First, and foremost, we must examine our own hearts. We need to see if we have any jealously, envy, strife, hatred, un-forgiveness or any other impure thoughts that may have led to the broken relationship. Also, we must examine ourselves to see if there is brokenness within us that needs to be healed before the brokenness causes damage to someone else. If we do, we need to pray a prayer of repentance to the Father, asking for forgiveness. Below is such a prayer.

Father,

In the name of my Lord and Savior Jesus Christ, I come before you thanking you for the opportunity to be in your presence once again. Father, thank you for allowing your son Jesus to come into this earth realm to serve as a redeemer for my sins. Father, it is because of your love for me that He came and shed His blood on Calvary's cross. Father, I thank you for the gift of forgiveness, and I am asking that you grant forgiveness unto me for harboring feelings of _____ in my heart. I know that this is what caused and/or contributed to the rift between me and _____. Lord, cleanse me from all impurities. I do not want to have evil and ungodly thoughts infiltrating my mind and turning my heart to stone. Father, I want to love all your creation from a pure heart. Father, strengthen me where I am weak and continue to show me where and how I contribute to discontentment in the lives of others as well as in my own life. Father, make me a whole person so that I may love others unconditionally. Father, do a new thing in me so that I may be the person you called me to be. I thank you in advance for your miraculous workmanship. In the name of Jesus I pray.

Amen.

Now here is a prayer for your loved one.

Mt 21:21	Father, I come before you in prayer and in faith.
Rom 13:11	Your Word says that now is the time for all to awaken from sleep.
Rom 13:11	For our salvation is nearer now than we first believed.
Col 1:13	Lord, deliver my loved ones from the power of

	darkness
Rom 13:12	and cause them to put on the armor of light.
Rom 13:14	Help them in their daily walk to put on the Lord Jesus Christ
Rom 13:13	and to avoid the lusts and idolatry of life.
Ps 119:37	Cause them to turn their eyes away from worthless things,
2Tim 2:26	to come to their senses, and escape the snare of the devil.
Rom 13:13	Deliver them from immorality, strife, and envy,
Heb 10:22	and draw them near to You, Father, with a true heart.
Mt 5:6	Create in them a hunger and thirst for You and Your righteousness,
Ps 119:37	and revive them in Your ways.
Col 1:9 I	ask that You fill them with the knowledge of Your will
Col 1:9	in all wisdom and spiritual understanding;
Col 1:10	that they might have a walk worthy of You, Lord,
Col 1:10	fully pleasing You, being fruitful in every good work,
Col 1:10	and increasing in the knowledge of You,
Col 1:11	strengthened with all might, according to Your glorious power.
Rom 8:30	Bring them into the calling that You have predestined for them;
1Chr 28:9	help them to serve You with a loyal heart and with a willing mind,
Ps 32:8	and instruct them in the way they should go.
Jas 1:22	Let them be doers of the Word and not hearers only,
Ps 119:97	meditating in Your Word day and night.
Ps 112:6	Establish their heart, so they will never be shaken,
1Cor 10:13	and show them a way of escape with every temptation.
Rom 13:8	Let them owe no man anything except their love.
1Jn 3:18	A love that is in deed and truth, not just in word and speech.
Ps 110:3	Let them be volunteers serving You in the time of Your power.
Mt 6:33	Seeking first Your kingdom so that they will reap

abundant blessings.

Prov 3:9	I pray that they will honor You with their possessions
Prov 3:9	and with the firstfruits of their increase;
Ps 111:1	Praising the Lord with their whole heart in the assembly
Ps 111:1	of the upright and in the congregation,
Mic 6:8	walking humbly with You Lord, being determined to act justly,
Ps 112:4	loving mercy and righteousness,
Ps 112:4	being gracious and full of compassion.

In Jesus' name,
Amen.

Only God can direct you in the area of a broken relationship or with a relationship that has its flaws. Others simply cannot do it, unless they hear from God about your situation. Most people, in an effort to assist, are always ready to give advice. I have found that every situation is unique and what works for one, may not work for another. Seek God for the answers you need for your relationship. He may send you to receive godly council from a specific person, He may even send a word to you, or He may reveal His message to you in His written word. Remember, God works in mysterious ways. The key is letting God be your guide, not your feelings, not your emotions, and not your intellect. My prayer is that your relationships will be healthy and productive.

Scriptures for Relationships

Proverbs 10:12 *Hatred stirreth up strifes: but love covereth all sins.*

Romans 13:10 *Love worketh no ill to his neighbour: therefore love is the fulfilling of the law.*

1 Peter 3:8-11 *Finally, be ye all of one mind, having compassion one of another, love as brethren, be pitiful, be courteous: Not rendering evil for evil, or railing for railing: but contrariwise blessing; knowing that ye are thereunto called, that ye should inherit a blessing. For he that will love life, and see good days, let him refrain his tongue from evil, and his lips that they speak no guile: Let him eschew evil, and do good; let him seek peace, and ensue it.*

1 Peter 1:22 *Seeing ye have purified your souls in obeying the truth through the spirit unto unfeigned love of the brethren, see that ye love one another with a pure heart fervently.*

1 Peter 3:1-7 *Likewise, ye wives, be in subjection to your own husbands; that, if any obey not the word, they also may without the word be won by the conversation of the wives; While they behold your chaste conversation coupled with fear. Whose adorning let it not be that outward adorning of plaiting the hair, and of wearing of gold, or of putting on of apparel; But let it be the hidden man of the heart, in that which is not corruptible, even the ornament of a meek and quiet spirit, which is in the sight of God of great price. For after this manner in the old time the holy women also, who trusted in God, adorned themselves, being in subjection unto their own husbands: Even as Sara obeyed Abraham, calling him lord: whose daughters ye are, as long as ye do well, and are not afraid with any amazement. Likewise, ye husbands, dwell with them according to knowledge, giving honour unto the wife, as*

unto the weaker vessel, and as being heirs together of the grace of life; that your prayers be not hindered.

Ephesians 4:31-32 *Let all bitterness, and wrath, and anger, and clamour, and evil speaking, be put away from you, with all malice: And be ye kind one to another, tenderhearted, forgiving one another, even as God for Christ's sake hath forgiven you.*

Glimmers of Hope

My Mother

My mom only had one eye. I hated her... she was such an embarrassment. She cooked for students and teachers to support the family. There was this one day during elementary school where my mom came to say hello to me. I was so embarrassed.

How could she do this to me? I ignored her, threw her a hateful look and ran out. The next day at school one of my classmates said, "EEEE, your mom only has one eye!"

I wanted to bury myself. I also wanted my mom to just disappear. I confronted her that day and said, "If you're only goanna make me a laughing stock, why don't you just die?" My mom did not respond... I didn't even stop to think for a second about what I had said, because I was full of anger. I was oblivious to her feelings.

I wanted out of that house and have nothing to do with her. So I studied real hard; I got a chance to go abroad to study. Then, I got married. I bought a house of my own. I had kids of my own. I was happy with my life, my kids and the comforts. Then one day, my mother came to visit me. She hadn't seen me in years and she had not even met her grandchildren. When she stood by the door, my children laughed at her, and I yelled at her for coming over uninvited. I screamed at her, "How dare you come to my house and scare my children!"
GET OUT OF HERE! NOW!!!"

And to this, my mother quietly answered, "Oh, I'm so sorry. I may have gotten the wrong address," and she disappeared out of sight.

One day, a letter regarding a school reunion came to my house. So I lied to my wife that I was going on a business trip.

After the reunion, I went to the old shack just out of curiosity. My neighbors said that she died. I did not shed a single tear. They handed me a letter that she had wanted me to have. "My dearest son, I think of you all the time. I'm sorry that I came to your house and scared your children. I was so glad when I heard you were coming for the reunion.

But I may not be able to even get out of bed to see you. I'm sorry that I was a constant embarrassment to you when you were growing up. You see........when you were very little, you got into an accident, and lost your eye. As a mother, I couldn't stand watching you having to grow up with one eye. So I gave you mine. I was so proud of my son who was seeing a whole new world for me, in my place, with that eye.

With all my love to you,

Your mother

My Brother's Keeper.......

A voyaging ship was wrecked during a storm at sea and only two of the men on it were able to swim to a small, desert-like island. The two survivors, not knowing what else to do, agreed that they had no other recourse but to pray to God. However, to find out whose prayer was more powerful, they agreed to divide the territory between them and stay on opposite sides of the island.

The first thing they prayed for was food. The next morning, the first man saw a fruit-bearing tree on his side of the land, and he was able to eat its fruit. The other man's parcel of land remained barren.

After a week, the first man was lonely and he decided to pray for a wife. The next day, another ship was wrecked, and the only survivor was a woman who swam to his side of the land. On the other side of the island, there was nothing.

Soon the first man prayed for a house, clothes, and more food. The next day, like magic, all of these were given to him. However, the second man still had nothing. Finally, the first man prayed for a ship, so that he and his wife could leave the island. In the morning, he found a ship docked at his side of the island. The first man boarded the ship with his wife and decided to leave the second man on the island. He considered the other man unworthy to receive God's blessings, since none of his prayers had been answered.

As the ship was about to leave, the first man heard a voice from heaven booming, "Why are you leaving your companion on the island?"

"My blessings are mine alone, since I was the one who prayed for them," the first man answered. "His prayers were all unanswered and so he does not deserve anything." "You are mistaken!" the voice rebuked him. "He had only one prayer, which I answered. If not for that, you would not have received any of my blessings."

"Tell me," the first man asked the voice, "what did he pray for that

I should owe him anything?"

"He prayed that all your prayers be answered." For all we know, our blessings are not the fruits of our prayers alone, but those of another praying for us.

When Jesus died on the cross He was thinking of you!

Six

Death

In the span of my 39 years of life, although death surrounds me daily on the news, with friends of friends, and with friends of family members, I have only experienced death up close and personal three times. Once was with a family member and twice with close friends. Experiencing death of a loved one can be very excruciating. Words fail to fully encapsulate the emotions that one experiences from the loss of a loved one. But God is able to comfort us as we go through the storm that death wants to settle upon us. In all three deaths that I experienced, my comfort came from the Lord.

When I was but 23 years old, I experienced the death of my best friend. Her name was Sabrina Walker and she was approximately three years younger than I was. She died just days before her twenty-first birthday. About eight years before her death, we both came to live in the city of Long Beach. We were from two different worlds, but found ourselves to be two peas in a pod. She grew up in the city of Long Beach where gangs and drug selling were very prominent and I grew up in a middle-class neighborhood in the city of Carson where news of gangs and drugs was non-existent (at that time).

However, at the age of 15, I found myself in the heart of Long Beach, and there I met Sabrina. As Long Beach wasn't really my cup of tea, directly after high school, I quickly moved to San Diego to attend college. In my absence, Sabrina and I lost touch for awhile. Later, I moved back to another part of Long Beach. During that time, I transferred to Long Beach State, got married and had my first son. Periodically, I would stop in to see Sabrina.

During our years of friendship, Sabrina and I were connected with some of the same people. One day, in the midst of final exams during my senior year in college, in May of 1992, I received a phone call from my sister-in-law. Her cousin, Nona, had called to tell her that my best friend Sabrina had died. That day, directly after school, I frantically drove to her mother's apartment looking for her. I had not been there in some time. When I arrived, to my surprise, the family had moved. However, someone recognized me and asked if I was looking for the Walker family. The person was gracious enough to give me the new address.

When I got there, I was even more shaken than when I got the news because I was sure that I would not be able to locate the right apartment and that I would not be able to see her mother and my goddaughter- Sabrina's daughter. Luckily, I found it. When I walked in, her mother took one look at me and said, "I didn't think you were going to know. I didn't think you were going to know." I told her that someone notified me. She looked at me and said, "You are the only true friend she ever had." And she just began to cry. I was astonished at her words because she had, for the most part, been very rude to me as if though I was the cause of her daughter living the life that she lived. But I was not. I knew nothing of the life of the "hood" prior to moving to the area. But, I guess as time went on, the truth about who I was eventually was revealed to Mrs. Walker.

The next day, the trip to view Sabrina's body was calm, for I did not truly know what I was in for. I had never viewed a body before, so I did not know what to expect. When I arrived at the funeral home, the director directed me to the room where her body was being held for viewing. At that point, I became nervous. I slowly entered the room, seeing the casket as I approached the open door. As I looked over into the casket, I could see that she had had other visitors because there were birthday cards all over her body. Actually, that is when I remembered that her birthday was approaching in less than a week. When I looked at her, I fell down into the chair that was placed right in front of the casket. I held my one-year-old son Aaron, that Sabrina never got a chance to meet, tightly to my chest and I wept.

I must have cried very hard and very loudly because the funeral director came in and asked if I was okay. He said that many had come to see her but no one had responded the way I did. He said, "You must have been very close to her." I told him, "She was my best friend." Every time I reminisce about that day, I think that I must have scared my son because he had never seen me respond that way before. He held on to me very tightly. He actually gave me comfort with his little arms. Just feeling the life inside of him was comforting. I am glad he was there. Unfortunately, I was unable to attend the funeral because it was scheduled at a time when I had a final exam. I was graduating with my bachelor's degree in a couple of weeks and could not miss any tests.

My friend Sabrina gave me many laughs and many adventures as she introduced me into her world. We experienced many great times and many dangerous times together. She will always have a place in my heart and in my memory. It is because of her that I understand things in life that I never experienced, like the loss of a child. Her second-born child was a still-born boy. I was by her side as she laid him to rest. Through good times and bad, we walked together sharing secrets. Sabrina Walker was wild and crazy, but she was my friend.

Four years later, in April of 1996, my maternal grandmother, by best friend of 28 years, took gravely ill. In months prior, she had been diagnosed with Hepatitis B. She had made many trips to the hospital because she was vomiting blood. The disease had attacked the lining of her stomach. One day as my mother and I were working, she cautiously looked up at me and said, "Granny is in the hospital again." I only nodded my head. We had experienced her being hospitalized at least twice before. But this time I had a different feeling about it.

Finally, after mulling over whether or not I should say what the Holy Spirit and given me an unction within my spirit to say, I spoke very cautiously, yet confidently to my mother, my grandmother's seventh child and fifth living daughter. I said, "You know she's not coming home this time." My mother softly replied, "I know."

When I went to visit my grandmother in the hospital, it was similar to my visit to Sabrina at the funeral home. I was not at all prepared for what I was about to see. When I entered the hospital room, my mother was standing at my grandmother's bedside talking to her. When I looked into the bed, I didn't see my grandmother. I didn't see my granny. I just saw a shell of who she used to be. My grandmother was 5'2" and weighed probably 130 pounds. The person who I could barely see in the bed was very small and thin. She looked to be about the size of a 10 year old. I immediately covered my mouth and started crying. My mother gently pushed me away from the bed and turned me toward the wall so that my grandmother could not see me. I collected myself and turned around. My mother smiled and asked me if I wanted to feed my grandmother some Jell-O. I nodded and commenced to giving Granny the Jell-O. She barely had enough strength to open her mouth. She looked at me with her little brown eyes that had a tinge of grey from the cataracts that was trying to attack them. After going through the painful process of watching her struggle to eat the soft substance, I had to excuse myself from the room. I went into the hallway and slowly leaned against the wall and slid down to the floor. I could not believe what I was witnessing. I was totally devastated.

Over the next days, I began to experience problems with my stomach that I had never experienced before. The pain that I felt told me that I had a hole inside of me. A part of me was missing and the physical part of it was never to return. The spirit-filled part would remain with me forever. A couple of days later, I decided to take my two sons, Aaron and Daron, who were six and three, to see their great grandmother. The night before I was to take them to the hospital, my phone rang and my aunt who was visiting from Arkansas was on the other end. She said, "Cassy, Granny's dead." I said, "Excuse me?" She said, "You heard what I said." I do not remember saying anything else. I just remember not being on the phone anymore. I was crushed. I already knew she was dying but I wanted my kids to say goodbye to her. Also, I could not believe that someone would be so crass to say what was said to me in the manner that it was said. I felt a little more love and care could have been used.

After hearing the brief, cut-and-dry statement that was said to me, I called my husband to come and get my kids, so I could go to the hospital. When I got there, many of my family members were there, in the hallway and all around her bed. This time when I saw her she looked more like herself, except she was swollen. Her stomach was full of air and was lifting the blanket up.

The granddaughter in me, who had just lost her best friend, wanted to scream and run out the room crying and throwing a tantrum throughout the hallways of the hospital. However, the mature adult that was being spirit led knew that she was in a better place and that she no longer suffered in her physical body. So, I leaned over and kissed her forehead and said something like, "It's over now Granny. Now you can rest."

Granny was truly my best friend. For years, as a teenage, I would spend my summers with Granny hanging out and studying God's word. We went to all the church services and events. Before getting married, I moved in with my granny for a year or so. Many people were shocked to find out that she was actually my grandmother and not my mother.

Although I had a tremendous amount of peace with the end of her suffering, it took me a long time before I stopped trying to pick up the phone and call her. We used to talk almost every day. There were times even now when I wish she was here to laugh with, talk to and get advice from. Unfortunately, she was not here to witness my graduation with my masters, nor will she be here to see me earn my two doctorates. She did not witness the release of any of my books, my minister licensing, or the ground breaking of my ministry. But what is more important to me is that she is in a better place, free from pain, cruelty and wickedness. She is with the master, but I know that she watches over me. I know I have had a least two visitations from her.

The most poignant one was when I was in New Orleans at the Hyatt. I had arrived there after fighting with my husband and sustaining a black eye. In the middle of the night, I got up to go to the restroom. As I turned the corner from the bed to approach the restroom, I saw my grandmother standing there in the corridor- live and in the flesh. I stopped in fright and surprise. She motioned for me to come to her, letting me know that it was okay. I stepped toward her knowing that she was going to disappear, only she did not disappear. She put her arms around me. Her hug was very comforting. It was as if she was telling me that all would be well. I then jumped up and found myself in bed. That experience was very surreal.

My third experience with death was the most recent one. It occurred during the writing of this book. This experience is really the one that precipitated the writing of this chapter. This experience really made me think about the finality of death. It caused me to examine who is currently in my life, the way life is lived, and what people choose to do with their lives as a whole. I usually do have these thoughts from time to time as this was one of the primary thought processes I had that initiated the writing of my book **Dare to Succeed by Breaking through Barriers.** I guess because I was a lot younger when Sabrina and Granny died, I did not think about death the same way that I did when my friend died in 2007.

As I was checking my email on Thursday November 8, 2007, I was surprised to see an email from my friend Tina. I knew that whatever it was about it must have been important because I almost never received an email from her. Then I looked at the subject line which read, "Gary's Dad." Without opening the email, I knew what it said, but I prayed any way. I was desperately hoping that the email said that he was only in the hospital and nothing worse. It took me two hours to find out what the email said due to a wavering internet connection. When I finally opened the email, it told a sad story. My friend of ten years, Pastor Willie Dixon, husband to Grace and father to Gary, Charm, and Zipporah, had passed. I was numb.

Sorrowfully, I told my son Daron first, who had spent countless days and nights at the Dixon home. He was concerned about his friend Gary. I was concerned about Grace and all of the children. During my friendship with Willie, I had developed a friendship with Grace as well. I remember stopping by their home for years after work one or two Fridays a month. I would pass their home on my way home from work. After visiting, I would always have to tear myself away to get home at a decent time. It was hard because we loved each others company. Willie was always there to give good advice, ask for my input on his projects, and just to laugh and talk with. He was truly precious and I will miss him tremendously. He is one of the few people that I have had the pleasure to call my friend.

As I told the attendees at Willie's funeral, I was very proud of him as he was the epitome of a fulfilled life, even though he died at the young age of 59. His life was definitely not lived in vain. His fulfilled his educational goals by earning two masters degrees; he had athletic goals of track and football that he accomplished; he desired to marry and have a family and he did. All that Willie desired and set his mind to do, he did. He never let obstacles get in his way and prevent him from attaining his goals. While obtaining his goals, he encouraged others to achieve theirs as well. In many respects, Willie and I were alike. We are both self-starters and encouragers of others.

In addition to all Willie's earthly accomplishments, he was a man of God. He preached and discussed the word of God with fervor. I believe this is what enabled him to always look at the bright side of life and to see the good in all situations no matter what it looked like on the surface. He walked by faith and set an example for others to do the same. He not only spoke the scriptures, but he lived them as well. His memory will live on forever as a man of integrity in the hearts of those who had the privilege to be graced with his presence.

In all my experiences with death, God gave me comfort and reached the hurting places that were in the depths of my soul. When the tears streamed from my eyes, His arms gave me comfort. When the words of loved ones attempted to comfort me and did not quite do the job, the spirit of the Lord enveloped me and gave me peace. My God was and is my comfort and my shield.

Now, let us examine the word of God. At the beginning of the book of Joshua, Joshua is found in mourning of his mentor and friend Moses, a servant of God, who has died. As a result of Moses' death, Joshua has been commanded to continue guiding the Israelites to the Promised Land. In doing so, he is also to divide the land amongst the twelve tribes. In chapter one verse two, God tells Joshua that his servant Moses is dead, but as Joshua is yet with the living, he has a job to do. Here we learn that although mourning is permissible, it is to last only for a season. We must continue to go about the Father's business as He as assigned to each of us. Let me remind you of the Great Commission as written in Matthew 28: 18-20 *"And Jesus came and spake unto them, saying, All power is given unto me in heaven and in earth. Go ye therefore, and teach all nations, baptizing them in the name of the Father, and of the Son, and of the Holy Ghost: Teaching them to observe all things whatsoever I have commanded you: and, lo, I am with you always, even unto the end of the world. Amen."*

Joshua, in respect to this commandment, was commanded to serve as a guide and a leader for the children of Israel. In chapter one verse nine, he is reminded of his responsibility. It states, *"Have not I commanded thee? Be strong and of a good courage; be not afraid, neither be thou dismayed: for the LORD thy God is with thee whithersoever thou goest."* God also ensures Joshua that He will be with him as he goes. He will be there every step of the way and He will not forsake him. God tells Joshua to be strong and of good courage. Physically, Joshua is fine; therefore, this statement refers to Joshua's emotional state. God is saying to keep the faith and do not buckle because a loved one has departed from this life. We must believe in who God created us to be. Those who mentor us will not always be with us.

In your time(s) of bereavement, remember that mourning is but for a season. We are not to focus on our loss of those who have passed from this life. Like Joshua, we must regroup and focus on our lives that we have left to live. We should ask ourselves the following questions: "When I face the Master will He say, 'Well done, my good and faithful servant'?" Have I answered the Master's call and been obedient to my calling?" "Have I reached the lost?"

Remember, death is our final act in this life. There is no turning back. But be of good courage; Isaiah 25:8 says that our Lord will swallow up death in victory. That means the saved will live on with Christ. We will see each other again. In this fact, we should rejoice.

Let us utter a word of prayer.

Dear Heavenly Father,

I thank you for your comfort in my times of bereavement, and I ask you to forgive me if I stayed in my mourning stage too long. I thank you for being my comfort, my peace, and my way maker. Thank you for allowing me to see the brightness of this day and for allowing me time to regain my focus on the assignments you have given me to complete during my lifetime. Father, I thank you for the strength to persevere. I know that I will still experience times of sadness as I reminisce on the fond memories I have of my loved one that departed this earth. But I know that you will comfort me and wipe my tears. I thank you that I can lift my head on this side of glory and continue to do your will, so that when my time comes to depart this earth I can see your face. I will continue to press on toward the mark for the prize of hearing you say, "Well done, my good and faithful servant."

In the name of Jesus I pray,

Amen.

How can I help someone I love?

Death is around us on a daily basis. It is an unavoidable fact of life. What people need most when they are in a period of bereavement is comfort. No one can take the place of the deceased person but sometimes having other loved ones around can serve as a comfort. The only thing I can suggest in the case of death is to release some of the burdens and tasks that the person may be facing, such as funeral arrangements, cooking, cleaning, finances, small children, dealing with family members, etc. Anything that you can do to relieve some of the immediate pressures, without causing more anxiety, will provide comfort to the individual. Remember, sometimes less is more. You do not want to get in the way. Some people just really want to be left alone so they can grieve in solitude and silence. Use the spirit of discernment to guide you. If the spirit of discernment is not working, just ask what help you can give and be sure to follow the instructions that are given.

Scriptures on Death

1 Thessalonians 4:13-14 *But I would not have you to be ignorant, brethren, concerning them which are asleep, that ye sorrow not, even as others which have no hope. For if we believe that Jesus died and rose again, even so them also which sleep in Jesus will God bring with him*

2 Thessalonians 2:16-17 *Now our Lord Jesus Christ himself, and God, even our Father, which hath loved us, and hath given us everlasting consolation and*

good hope through grace, Comfort your hearts, and establish you in every good word and work.

Matthew 5:4 *Blessed are they that mourn: for they shall be comforted.*

2 Corinthians 1:3-4 *Blessed be God, even the Father of our Lord Jesus Christ, the Father of mercies, and the God of all comfort; Who comforteth us in all our tribulation, that we may be able to comfort them which are in any trouble, by the comfort wherewith we ourselves are comforted of God.*

2 Corinthians 5:8 *We are confident, I say, and willing rather to be absent from the body, and to be present with the Lord.*

Psalms 119:50 *This is my comfort in my affliction: for thy word hath quickened me.*

Psalm 23 *Yea, though I walk through the valley of the shadow of death, I will fear no evil: for thou art with me; thy rod and thy staff they comfort me.*

Isaiah 49:13b *for the Lord hath comforted his people, and will have mercy upon his afflicted.*

Isaiah 61:1-3 *The Spirit of the Lord God is upon me; because the Lord hath anointed me to preach good tidings unto the meek; he hath sent me to bind up the brokenhearted, to proclaim liberty to the captives, and the opening of the prison to them that are bound; To proclaim the acceptable year of the Lord, and the day of vengeance of our God; to comfort all that mourn; To appoint unto them that mourn in Zion, to give unto them beauty for ashes, the oil of joy for mourning, the garment of praise for the spirit of heaviness; that they might be called trees of righteousness, the planting of the Lord, that he might be glorified.*

Isaiah 41:10 *Fear thou not; for I am with thee: be not dismayed; for I am thy God: I will strengthen thee; yea, I will help thee; yea, I will uphold thee with the right hand of my righteousness.*

Isaiah 51:11 *Therefore the redeemed of the Lord shall return, and come with singing unto Zion; and everlasting joy shall be upon their head: they shall obtain gladness and joy; and sorrow and mourning shall flee away.*

1 Peter 5:7 *Casting all your care upon him; for he careth for you.*

1 Corinthians 15:55-57 *O death, where is thy sting? O grave, where is thy victory? The sting of death is sin; and the strength of sin is the law. But thanks be to God, which giveth us the victory through our Lord Jesus Christ.*

Revelations 21:4 *And God shall wipe away all tears from their eyes; and there shall be no more death, neither sorrow, nor crying, neither shall there be any more pain: for the former things are passed away.*

Through the Storm   C. White-Elliott

Glimmers of Hope

Two Choices

At a fundraising dinner for a school that serves learning-disabled children, the father of one of the students delivered a speech that would never be forgotten by all who attended. After extolling the school and its dedicated staff, he offered a question: "When not interfered with by outside influences, everything nature does is done with perfection. Yet my son, Shay, cannot learn things as other children do. He cannot understand things as other children do. Where is the natural order of things in my son?" The audience was stilled by the query.

The father continued. "I believe that when a child like Shay, physically and mentally handicapped comes into the world, an opportunity to realize true human nature presents itself, and it comes in the way other people treat that child." Then he told the following story:

Shay and his father had walked past a park where some boys Shay knew were playing baseball. Shay asked, "Do you think they'll let me play?" Shay's father knew that most of the boys would not want someone like Shay on their team, but the father also understood that if his son were allowed to play, it would give him a much-needed sense of belonging and some confidence to be accepted by others in spite of his handicaps.

Shay's father approached one of the boys on the field and asked (not expecting much) if Shay could play. The boy looked around for guidance and said, "We're losing by six runs and the game is in the eighth inning. I guess he can be on our team and we'll try to put him in to bat in the ninth inning."

Shay struggled over to the team's bench and, with a broad smile, put on a team shirt. His father watched with a small tear in his eye and warmth in his heart. The boys saw the father's joy at his son being accepted. In the bottom of the eighth inning, Shay's team scored a few runs but was still behind by three. In the top of the ninth inning, Shay put on a glove and played in the right field. Even though no hits came his way, he was obviously ecstatic just to be in the game and on the field, grinning from ear to ear as his father waved to him from the stands. In the bottom of the ninth inning, Shay's team scored again. Now, with two outs and the bases loaded, the potential winning run was on base and Shay was scheduled to be next at bat.

At this juncture, do they let Shay bat and give away their chance to win the game? Surprisingly, Shay was given the bat. Everyone knew that a hit was all but impossible because Shay didn't even know how to hold the bat properly, much less connect with the ball.

However, as Shay stepped up to the plate, the pitcher, recognizing that the other team was putting winning aside for this moment in Shay's life, moved in a few steps to lob the ball in softly so Shay could at least make contact. The first pitch came and Shay swung clumsily and missed.

The pitcher again took a few steps forward to toss the ball softly towards Shay. As the pitch came in, Shay swung at the ball and hit a slow ground ball right back to the pitcher. The game would now be over. The pitcher picked up the soft grounder and could have easily thrown the ball to the first baseman. Shay would have been out and that would have been the end of the game.

Instead, the pitcher threw the ball right over the first baseman's head, out of reach of all team mates. Everyone from the stands and both teams started yelling, "Shay, run to first! Run to first!" Never in his life had Shay ever run that far, but he made it to first base.

He scampered down the baseline, wide-eyed and startled. Everyone yelled, "Run to second, run to second!" Catching his breath, Shay awkwardly ran towards second, gleaming and struggling to make it to the base. By the time Shay rounded towards second base, the right fielder had the ball ... the smallest guy on their team who now had his first chance to be the hero for his team. He could have thrown the ball to the second-baseman for the tag, but he understood the pitcher's intentions so he, too, intentionally threw the ball high and far over the third-baseman's head. Shay ran toward third base deliriously as the runners ahead of him circled the bases toward home.

All were screaming, "Shay, Shay, Shay, all the way Shay." Shay reached third base because the opposing shortstop ran to help him by turning him in the direction of third base, and shouted, "Run to third! Shay, run to third!" As Shay rounded third, the boys from both teams, and the spectators, were on their feet screaming, "Shay, run home! Run home!" Shay ran to home, stepped on the plate, and was cheered as the hero who hit the grand slam and won the game for his team. "That day," said the father softly with tears now rolling down his face, "the boys from both teams helped bring a piece of true love and humanity into this world."

Shay didn't make it to another summer. He died that winter, having never forgotten being the hero and making his father so happy and coming home and seeing his mother tearfully embrace her little hero of the day!

Gone but Not Forgotten

Jack took a long look at his speedometer before slowing down: 73 in a 55 zone. Fourth time in as many months. How could a guy get caught so often? When his car had slowed to 10 miles an hour, Jack pulled over, but only partially. Let the cop worry about the potential traffic hazard. Maybe some other car will tweak his backside with a mirror. The cop was stepping out of his car, the big pad in hand.

Bob? Bob from Church? Jack sunk farther into his trench coat. This was worse than the coming ticket. A cop catching a guy from his own church. A guy who happened to be a little eager to get home after a long day at the office. A guy he was about to play golf with tomorrow. Jumping out of the car, he approached a man he saw every Sunday, a man he'd never seen in uniform. "Hi, Bob. Fancy meeting you like this." "Hello, Jack." No smile.

"Guess you caught me red-handed in a rush to see my wife and kids."

"Yeah, I guess." Bob seemed uncertain. Good.

"I've seen some long days at the office lately. I'm afraid I bent the rules a bit -just this once."

Jack toed at a pebble on the pavement. "Diane said something about roast beef and potatoes tonight. Know what I mean?" "I know what you mean. I also know that you have a reputation in our precinct." Ouch. This was not going in the right direction. Time to change tactics. "What'd you clock me at?" "Seventy. Would you sit back in your car please?" "Now wait a minute here, Bob. I checked as soon as I saw you. I was barely nudging 65." The lie seemed to come easier with every ticket.

"Please, Jack, in the car."

Flustered, Jack hunched himself through the still-open door. Slamming it shut, he stared at the dashboard. He was in no rush to open the window. The minutes ticked by. Bob scribbled away on the pad. Why hadn't he asked for a driver's license? Whatever the reason, it would be a month of Sundays before Jack ever sat near this cop again. A tap on the door jerked his head to the left. There was Bob, a folded paper in hand Jack rolled down the window a mere two inches, just enough room for Bob to pass him the slip. "Thanks." Jack could not quite keep the sneer out of his voice. Bob returned to his police car without a word. Jack watched his retreat in the mirror. Jack unfolded the sheet of paper. How much was this one going to cost? Wait a minute. What was this? Some kind of joke? Certainly not a ticket.

Jack began to read: "Dear Jack, Once upon a time I had a daughter. She was six when killed by a car. You guessed it- a speeding driver. A fine and three months in jail, and the man was free. Free to hug his daughters, all three of them. I only had one, and I'm going to have to wait until Heaven before I can ever hug her again. A thousand times I've tried to forgive that man. A thousand times I thought I had. Maybe I did, but I need to do it again. Even now. Pray for me. And be careful, Jack, my son is all I have left."

"Bob"

Jack turned around in time to see Bob's car pull away and head down the road. Jack watched until it disappeared. A full 15 minutes later, he too, pulled away and drove slowly home, praying for forgiveness and hugging a surprised wife and kids when he arrived.

Life is precious. Handle with care.

The Room

17-year-old Brian Moore had only a short time to write something for a class. The subject was "What Heaven was Like." "I wowed 'em," he later told his father, Bruce. "It's a killer. It's the bomb. It's the best thing I ever wrote." It also was the last.

Brian's parents had forgotten about the essay when a cousin found it while cleaning out the teenager's locker at Teary Valley High School. Brian had been dead only hours, but his parents desperately wanted every piece of his life near them-notes from classmates and teachers, his homework.

Only two months before, he had handwritten the essay about encountering Jesus in a file room full of cards detailing every moment of the teen's life. But it was only after Brian's death that Beth and Bruce Moore realized that their son had described his view of heaven. "It makes such an impact that people want to share it. You feel like you are there," Mr. Moore said.

Brian Moore died May 27, 1997, the day after Memorial Day. He was driving home from a friend's house when his car went off Bulen-Pierce Road in Pickaway County and struck a utility pole. He emerged from the wreck unharmed but stepped on a downed power line and was electrocuted.

The Moores framed a copy of Brian's essay and hung it among the family portraits in the living room. "I think God used him to make a point. I think we were meant to find it and make something out of it," Mrs. Moore said of the essay. She and her husband wanted to share their son's vision of life after death. "I'm happy for Brian. I know he's in heaven. I know I'll see him."

Brian's Essay: The Room...

In that place between wakefulness and dreams, I found myself in the room. There were no distinguishing features except for the one wall covered with small index card files. They were like the ones in libraries that list titles by author or subject in alphabetical order. But these files, which stretched from floor to ceiling and seemingly endless in either direction, had very different headings. As I drew near the wall of files, the first to catch my attention was one that read "Girls I have liked." I opened it and began flipping through the cards. I quickly shut it, shocked to realize that I recognized the names written on each one. And then without being told, I knew exactly where I was.

This lifeless room with its small files was a crude catalog system for my life. Here were written the actions of my every moment, big and small, in a detail my memory couldn't match. A sense of wonder and curiosity, coupled with horror, stirred within me as I began randomly opening files and exploring their content. Some brought joy and sweet memories; others brought a sense of shame and regret so intense that I would look over my shoulder to see if anyone was watching.

A file named "Friends" was next to one marked "Friends I Have Betrayed." The titles arranged from the mundane to the outright weird "Books I Have Read," "Lies I Have Told," "Comfort I Have Given," "Jokes I Have Laughed At." Some were almost hilarious in their exactness: "Things I've Yelled at My Brothers." Others I couldn't laugh at: "Things I Have Done in My Anger", "Things I Have Muttered Under My Breath at My Parents." I never ceased to be surprised by the contents. Often there were many more cards than I expected. Sometimes fewer than I hoped. I was overwhelmed by the sheer volume of the life I had lived. Could it be possible that I had the time in my years to fill each of these thousands or even millions of cards? But each card confirmed this truth. Each was written in my own handwriting. Each signed with my signature.

When I pulled out the file marked "TV Shows I have watched," I realized the files grew to contain their contents. The cards were packed tightly, and yet after two or three yards, I hadn't found the end of the file. I shut it, shamed, not so much by the quality of shows but more by the vast time I knew that file represented.

When I came to a file marked "Lustful Thoughts," I felt a chill run through my body. I pulled the file out only an inch, not willing to test its size and drew out a card. I shuddered at its detailed content. I felt sick to think that such a moment had been recorded. An almost animal rage broke in me. One thought dominated my mind: No one must ever see these cards! No one must ever see this room! I have to destroy them!" In insane frenzy, I yanked the file out. Its size didn't matter now. I had to empty it and burn the cards. But as I took it at one end and began pounding it on the floor, I could not dislodge a single card. I became desperate and pulled out a card, only to find it as strong as steel when I tried to tear it.

Defeated and utterly helpless, I returned the file to its slot. Leaning my forehead against the wall, I let out a long, self-pitying sigh. And then I saw it. The title bore "People I Have Shared the Gospel With." The handle was brighter than those around it, newer, almost unused. I pulled on its handle and a small box not more than three inches long fell into my hands. I could count the cards it contained on one hand.

And then the tears came. I began to weep. Sobs so deep that they hurt. They started in my stomach and shook through me. I fell on my knees and cried. I cried out of shame, from the overwhelming shame of it all. The rows of file shelves swirled in my tear-filled eyes. No one must ever, ever know of this room. I must lock it up and hide the key. But then as I pushed away the tears, I saw Him.

No, please not Him. Not here. Oh, anyone but Jesus. I watched helplessly as He began to open the files and read the cards. I couldn't bear to watch His response. And in the moments I could bring myself to look at His face, I saw a sorrow deeper than my own. He seemed to intuitively go to the worst boxes. Why did He have to read every one? Finally, He turned and looked at me from across the room. He looked at me with pity in His eyes. But this was a pity that didn't anger me. I dropped my head, covered my face with my hands and began to cry again. He walked over and put His arm around me. He could have said so many things. But He didn't say a word. He just cried with me.

Then He got up and walked back to the wall of files. Starting at one end of the room, He took out a file and, one by one, began to sign His name over mine on each card. "No!" I shouted rushing to Him. All I could find to say was "No, no," as I pulled the card from Him. His name shouldn't be on these cards. But there it was, written in red so rich, so dark, so alive. The name of Jesus covered mine. It was written with His blood. He gently took the card back. He smiled a sad smile and began to sign the cards. I don't think I'll ever understand how He did it so quickly, but the next instant it seemed I heard Him close the last file and walk back to my side.

He placed His hand on my shoulder and said, "It is finished." I stood up, and He led me out of the room. There was no lock on its door. There were still cards to be written.

"I can do all things through Christ who strengthens me."-Phil. 4:13

"For God so loved the world that He gave His only son, that whoever believes in Him shall not perish but have eternal life." - John 3:16

Scars of Love

Some years ago, on a hot summer day in south Florida, a little boy decided to go for a swim in the old swimming hole behind his house. In a hurry to dive into the cool water, he ran out the back door, leaving behind shoes, socks, and shirt as he went.

He flew into the water, not realizing that as he swam toward the middle of the lake, an alligator was swimming toward the shore. His father working in the yard saw the two as they got closer and closer together. In utter fear, he ran toward the water, yelling to his son as loudly as he could.

Hearing his voice, the little boy became alarmed and made a U-turn to swim to his father. It was too late. Just as he reached his father, the alligator reached him. From the dock, the father grabbed his little boy by the arms just as the alligator snatched his legs. That began an incredible tug-of-war between the two. The alligator was much stronger than the father, but the father was much too passionate to let go. A farmer happened to drive by, heard his screams, raced from his truck, took aim and shot the alligator.

Remarkably, after weeks and weeks in the hospital, the little boy survived. His legs were extremely scarred by the vicious attack of the animal. And, on his arms, were deep scratches where his father's fingernails dug into his flesh in his effort to hang on to the son he loved.

The newspaper reporter who interviewed the boy after the trauma, asked if he would show him his scars. The boy lifted his pant legs. And then, with obvious pride, he said to the reporter, "But look at my arms. I have great scars on my arms, too. I have them because my Dad wouldn't let go."

You and I can identify with that little boy. We have scars, too. No, not from an alligator, but the scars of a painful past. Some of those scars are unsightly and have caused us deep regret. But, some wounds, my friend, are because God has refused to let go. In the midst of your struggle, He's been there holding on to you.

The Scripture teaches that God loves you. You are a child of God He wants to protect you and provide for you in every way. But sometimes we foolishly wade into dangerous situations, not knowing what lies ahead. The swimming hole of life is filled with peril - and we forget that the enemy is waiting to attack. That's when the tug-of-war begins - and if you have the scars of His love on your arms, be very, very grateful. He did not and will not ever let you go.

God has blessed you, so that you can be a blessing to others. You just never know where a person is in his/her life and what they are going through. Never judge another person's scars, because you don't know how they got them. Right now, someone needs to know that God loves them, and you love them, too- enough to not let them go.

Sometimes it is instances of a near-death experience that makes people really value life. Don't let the end draw near before you tell a loved one how you feel. Demonstrate it with every breath you take.

Positive Mental Attitude!!

We can all learn a lesson from this great old girl!

The 92-year-old, petite, well-poised and proud lady, who is fully dressed each morning by eight o'clock, with her hair fashionably coifed and makeup perfectly applied, even though she is legally blind, moved to a nursing home today. Her husband of 70 years recently passed away, making the move necessary.

After many hours of waiting patiently in the lobby of the nursing home, she smiled sweetly when told her room was ready. As she maneuvered her walker to the elevator, I provided a visual description of her tiny room, including the eyelet sheets that had been hung on her window.

"I love it," she stated with the enthusiasm of an eight-year-old having just been presented with a new puppy.

"Mrs. Jones, you haven't seen the room. Just wait."

"That doesn't have anything to do with it," she replied. "Happiness is something you decide on ahead of time. Whether I like my room or not doesn't depend on how the furniture is arranged... it's how I arrange my mind. I already decided to love it "It's a decision I make every morning when I wake up. I have a choice; I can spend the day in bed recounting the difficulty I have with the parts of my body that no longer work, or get out of bed and be thankful for the ones that do. Each day is a gift, and as long as my eyes open I'll focus on the new day and all the happy memories I've stored away .just for this time in my life.

There is life after a loved one passes from this life. Old age is like a bank account. You withdraw from what you've put in. So, my advice to you would be to deposit a lot of happiness in the bank account of memories.

Remember the five simple rules to be happy:

1. Free your heart from hatred.
2. Free your mind from worries.
3. Live simply.
4. Give more.
5. Expect less.

Seven

Regaining a Loss

Brought to You by the Help of the Brilliant Mind of Daron White

There are times in life when we work hard to obtain the desires of our hearts. Our desires may range from a position at work, a relationship with a spouse, person of interest or our children, a position on a team, to a number of other things. However, there are occasions when we get a grasp on our desire and we can feel the warmth of it in our hands, but our desires sometimes have a tendency to slip away from us if we become careless, neglectful, cocky, or arrogant. We should always cherish what God blesses us with and we should recognize the value that it has. When we fail to do this, God may allow the enemy to come in and rob from us a valued treasure. For some who have lost their hearts desire, they did not see the real value of it until it was gone. But, if they are doubly blessed, they may get another opportunity to earn it again. Will they value the treasure the next time or will they falter once again? In this chapter, we will survey various examples of those who gained and lost.

Anybody for a Game of Football?

Let us take, for example, the case of a high school freshman football player. At the beginning of the football season, he found himself working really hard to gain a starting position as cornerback. After long strenuous hours of practice, which were held four days a week, he was awarded the positioned he longed for. After only two weeks of serving in the starting position, he had to take a trip out of town with his family. When he came back, he found that his position was taken away and he was no longer a starting player. He found that his loss was due primarily to failing to communicate with his coach. In preparing for his trip, he neglected to tell his coach that he would miss practice for a week and would also miss one game.

In an effort to get his position back, he struggled for two and a half weeks, taking extra notes while watching the football films, watching professional football games, being anxious to get to practice, and running extra bleachers on the weekend to increase his durability and stamina. At the end of all his over zealous efforts, he regained his starting position with only two games left in the season. He was ecstatic. At the second to last game, he scored three touchdowns, had five interceptions, ran a total of 48 yards, and had five tackles. In the final game of the season, he had five deflections, made five tackles, inflicted one forced fumble, and scored the winning touchdown off an interception.

This young football player learned that the true meaning of teamwork is communicating with one another so that all parties will know what is going on and they can act accordingly. He had gone off on his on accord thinking that everything would be the same when he returned. He was in for a rude awakening. He learned that the team did not revolve around him, but each member of the team had to work together in order for them to be the undefeated team that they were at the end of the season. Now, he is anxiously looking forward to being a team player next year when he plays for the junior varsity and varsity teams.

A Woman Gone Wild

While a woman had been working at a company for over ten years, she had continuously moved up the chain of command. However, her desire was to earn the position of vice president. Finally after years of dedicated and loyal service, she earned her heart's desire. Her hard work and perseverance paid off. But, after working in her new position for only a few months, she became insolent. She no longer put in the long hours or offered the same dedication. As time drew on, she began to slack off more and more as she grew more and more comfortable with her newfound success.

Finally, her boss was fed up with her and he eventually found a replacement for her position. She was totally devastated. When she began to look back over her career, all she could say was that it was no one's fault but her own. She had worked hard to get to where she was, but then somewhere along the way, she lost sight of what was important. She learned that just as she had valued the position before she was in it, she should have continued to value it when she earned it. She learned that she never truly valued her job until it was gone.

Grades Gone Awry

A happy-go-lucky eighth grader, at the constant persistence of his mother, began to earnestly strive to get better grades than he had ever attained before. From his own desires, he wanted to earn a 4.0. So he studied and studied until he reached his goal. At the end of the first semester, he had indeed earned a 4.0. He had an A in every class. During the Christmas break, he bragged to everyone about his 4.0. As he bragged, he moved from being confident to being cocky. He even teased his older brother by saying that he is smarter than his brother is. When the next semester began, the lofty teenager did not continue with the study habits that he had developed. Instead, he started to slack off in doing his homework because he believed that it was his brain power and not his study habits that contributed to his 4.0.

At the end of the third quarter, to his dismay, he no longer had a 4.0. He missed it by one point. Instead of a 4.0 he earned a 3.9, for he had earned a B+ in one of his classes instead of an A. After seeing the error of his ways, he began to study harder. As a result of his determination and perseverance, he regained his 4.0 at the end of the school year. Not only did he live up to his mother's expectations, but he lived up to his own. He learned that rather than bragging about his achievements, he needs to work hard to maintain them in order to hold onto them.

Is This my Soul Mate?

Here is the case of Robert and Vanessa. Robert was always interested in Vanessa for as long as he could remember. They went to high school together and even attended the same college. Try as he might, Vanessa would not go out with Robert. Finally, after another three years, Robert and Vanessa began working at the same law firm. When they reconnected, Vanessa began to see Robert in a new light. He seemed to be more serious about life, more handsome, and even more humorous. After a few requests to have dinner after work, Vanessa finally accepted Robert's invitation. This was the start of a life-long relationship Robert thought. When the relationship began, Robert had flowers sent to Vanessa's office and would drop off just-because gifts to her at least once a week. Vanessa even found herself doing special things for Robert that went up and beyond the norm of what a new couple usually does. Things were going well.

After about a few months, Robert began to believe that nothing could go wrong. He felt that this relationship with Vanessa that he had desired for so long was "in the bag." He stopped paying as much attention to her and even missed some of their regular Wednesday night dates. He also began to forget to return calls. After awhile,

Vanessa began to question whether or not she should have given Robert a chance in the first place. After a few weeks of his nonchalant attitude, Vanessa decided she could take no more. Robert gave her no explanation about his change in behavior, so she decided it would be better if they did not pursue their relationship any longer.

The reality of Vanessa's decision must have been so shocking to Robert that he immediately began to mentally rewind the last month. He saw that he did the very things that Vanessa said he did. He tried to figure out what caused him to behave in such a manner. Did he really take her for granted or was the pressure of the cases he was working on wearing on him? He could not place his finger on it. All he knew was that he did not want to be without Vanessa. He was convinced that they were soul mates.

After about three weeks of trying to convince Vanessa that they should start over, he felt like he was going down memory lane. He felt like he was back in high school and college when he was always trying to get Vanessa to go out with him. He asked himself repeatedly, "How did I get back here?" Finally, Vanessa consented to giving the relationship another try. Today, they are married with two beautiful children, Dominique and Shaneice. Robert learned that when he values someone, he should always let the person know how precious he/she is and work hard to keep the relationship in good standing.

A Thin Line Crosse

Michael, a single father of two boys, after his divorce and custody battle, dreadfully faces the reality that he has an anger problem. One day when the boys were visiting their mother, the mother noticed bruising on the boys' legs and backs. She decided to sue for custody even though she lost the first custody case. With the proof that she submitted to the court, the judge awarded her full custody of her sons. After having the children live with her for a few weeks, she decided to get them counseling. This helped when time came for the children to visit their father. They were frightened that something they might do would set him off.

After seeing the damage that he had done to his sons, Michael decided to go into a treatment program. Shortly after completing his twelve-step program, he decided to file for joint custody of his children. Seeing Michael's attempt to better himself, the judge granted his request but also insisted that he attend regular AA meetings.

Life seemed to be evenly balanced at this point. The children were spending equal time with their mother and father and all parties seemed to be doing well. After about six months, things began to look gloomy. After a hard days work, Michael decided to go out for drinks with some friends, thinking he had control over the alcohol. Later that night, after returning home and releasing the babysitter, Michael began to yell at one of his sons for spilling juice on the carpet. Once again, Michael went overboard with his disciplining. He hit his son too hard.

Once again his ex-wife learned of what happened and again filed for sole custody of the boys. Again her request was granted. Michael is now only permitted to see his children once a week, and that visit is to be supervised. Michael learned that even though his twelve-step program taught him methods to deal with his anger, he found that drinking alcohol gave him less control over his actions. He learned that certain behaviors and tendencies do not mix. Today, he is still learning to control his anger and he is doing so without drinking. He decided that this step was the best choice in order to restore his relationship with his sons.

Just as we can examine modern examples of people suffering losses that they hope to regain, we can survey the bible for just as many examples. Looking at the New Testament, Jesus uses many examples of people losing their treasures when he shares his parables. Three parables that have come to be commonly titled as the Lost Parables are The Lost Coin, The Lost Sheep and the Lost Son (The Prodigal Son). "The Lost Son" is a parable that Jesus uses to explicate and demonstrate the importance of saving souls- the lost. Through this parable and the others, He demonstrates that God is concerned about all of us, and that He wishes that none will perish (2 Peter 3:9).

The parable of "The Lost Son" ironically includes relationship issues. Many who discuss the inherent broken relationship usually survey it from the father's perspective. This has resulted in the title of "The Lost Son." They focus on the father having two sons: one who remained home and the other who left home to seek out a better, more fulfilled life. For the purpose of this chapter, let us examine the father/son relationship from the alternate perspective. Looking at the relationship from the son's perspective, the son was blessed by God to live in a stable home that was filled with love, support, and guidance from his father. Rather than remaining there and continuing to flourish, he decided to request his inheritance early from his father so that he could seek out a life that was more to his liking.

At the beginning, the son was totally enthralled was his life and did not take a second look back at the life he left behind. However, his perception of life away from his family changed when his money ran out and he found himself eating with the pigs. At this point, he began to value the family that he was so richly blessed with. As a result, he humbled himself and returned home in an effort to regain the relationship with his father and family that he so foolishly abandoned. As an added blessing, he received, for a second time, more than he even thought to ask. His father awaited his return with open arms.

From all the scenarios included in this chapter, we can see that losses can sometimes come as storms in our lives when they disrupt our everyday life that we have become accustomed to. In an effort to prevent a storm of this nature, we should be careful to examine our relationships and our positions in life. We should be careful to not take for granted all that God has blessed us with. And we should be careful to give God all of the honor, the praise, and the glory that is due to Him.

If you have found yourself trying to regain things or relationships that you have lost, pray the following prayer.

Heavenly Father,

You have blessed me with so much during my short time here on earth. I know you did not have to do it, but you did because of the love that you have for me. I have been blessed with loved ones, food, and shelter. I have accumulated things that other people have only desired to have. At the same time, I have taken some things for granted. I have not cherished everything you have given me. As a result, some things have become out of my reach. Father God, I repent for my carefree attitude. I pray Lord that you will forgive me and afford me an opportunity to regain that which I have lost. I know that it was a blessing when you gave it to me. I will honor you and cherish your gifts as the blessings that they are from this point forward. If I need to make corrections in my life, I pray that you will reveal to me my shortcomings and give me an opportunity to get it right. Strengthen me oh Lord in the areas where I am weak. Make me strong. Show me how to be an over comer. Lord, I thank you in advance for what you are going to do on my behalf.

In the name of Jesus, my Lord and Savior,

Amen.

How can I help someone I love?

When you witness the saints of God taking God's blessings for granted or taking credit for their successes, you may need to give them a gentle nudge reminding them of God's love and kindness. This is not about sending them on a guilt trip; it is to remind them that we do not operate independently without the Father. You might say something like, "Wow, God really is showing out in your life. What a blessing it is to receive a new car, or a promotion on your job, or the release of a new cd (whatever the blessing may be). You are really an example of what God can do in the life of His children." Most times than not, the person will begin to praise God with you. What has transpired here is a friendly reminder of who truly is in control of everything and that we can do nothing on our own. No guilt trip was laid on the person; instead, he/she was encouraged to give God the praise that was due to Him and to offer words of thanksgiving. This simple act can keep a person from foolishly loosing what God has blessed him or her with. It can make all the difference in how situations are viewed and how they turn out.

Say this prayer to the Father if you desire to help others.

Father God,

Thank you for allowing me to know that you are the giver of all gifts, no matter their size. Thank you for allowing me to see you at work in my life and in the lives of others. Father, I want to acknowledge you for all that you do in my life and I want to help remind others of who you are and what you do daily to give us a better life than we could give to ourselves. Sometimes we are blinded by our success, but we truly mean no harm nor any disrespect to you, Father. Father, before anyone looses the blessings that you have been so gracious to provide, allow me an opportunity to remind them of their source of blessings. I am sure that they will be so careful to give you all the honor, praise and glory that is due to you.

In Jesus' name I pray,

Amen.

Scriptures for Losses

Galatians 6:9 *And let us not be weary in well doing: for in due season we shall reap, if we faint not.*

Psalm 31:24 *Be of good courage, and he shall strengthen your heart, all ye that hope in the Lord.*

Hebrews 10:35-36 *Cast not away therefore your confidence, which hath great recompence of reward. For ye have need of patience, that, after ye have done the will of God, ye might receive the promise.*

John 14:1 *Let not your heart be troubled: ye believe in God, believe also in me.*

Glimmers of Hope

Satan's Convention

"We can't keep Christians from going to church."

"We can't keep them from reading their Bibles and knowing the truth."

"We can't even keep them from forming an intimate relationship with their Saviour."

"Once they gain that connection with Jesus, our power over them is broken."

"So let them go to their churches; let them have their covered dish dinners, BUT steal their time, so they don't have time to develop a relationship with Jesus Christ."

"This is what I want you to do," said the devil:

"Distract them from gaining hold of their Saviour and maintaining that vital connection throughout their day!"

"How shall we do this?" his demons shouted.

"Keep them busy in the non-essentials of life and invent innumerable schemes to occupy their minds," he answered.

"Tempt them to spend, spend, spend, and borrow, borrow, borrow."

"Persuade the wives to go to work for long hours and the husbands to work 6-7 days each week, 10-12 hours a day, so they can afford their empty lifestyles."

"Keep them from spending time with their children."

"As their families fragment, soon, their homes will offer no escape from the pressures of work!"

"Over-stimulate their minds so that they cannot hear that still, small voice."

"Entice them to play the radio or cassette player whenever they drive."

To keep the TV, VCR, CDs and their PCs going constantly in their home and see to it that every store and restaurant in the world plays non-biblical music constantly."

"This will jam their minds and break that union with Christ."

"Fill the coffee tables with magazines and newspapers."

"Pound their minds with the news 24 hours a day."

"Invade their driving moments with billboards."

"Flood their mailboxes with junk mail, mail order catalogs, sweepstakes, and every kind of newsletter and promotional offering free products, services and false hopes."

"Keep skinny, beautiful models on the magazines and TV so their husbands will believe that outward beauty is what's important, and they'll become dissatisfied with their wives."

"Keep the wives too tired to love their husbands at night."

"Give them headaches too!"

"If they don't give their husbands the love they need, they will begin to look elsewhere."

"That will fragment their families quickly!"

"Give them Santa Claus to distract them from teaching their children the real meaning of Christmas."

"Give them an Easter bunny, so they won't talk about His resurrection and power over sin and death."

"Even in their recreation, let them be excessive."

"Have them return from their recreation exhausted."

"Keep them too busy to go out in nature and reflect on God's creation. Send them to amusement parks, sporting events, plays, concerts, and movies instead."

"Keep them busy, busy, busy!"

"And when they meet for spiritual fellowship, involve them in gossip and small talk so that they leave with troubled consciences."

"Crowd their lives with so many good causes they have no time to seek power from Jesus."

"Soon they will be working in their own strength, sacrificing their health and family for the good of the cause."

"It will work!"

"It will work!"

It was quite a plan!

The demons went eagerly to their assignments causing Christians everywhere to get busier and more rushed, going here and there. Having little time for their God or their families.

Having no time to tell others about the power of Jesus to change lives.

I guess the question is, has the devil been successful in his schemes?

This discussion includes all the reasons why we lose focus of what God has blessed us with: Him, loved ones, jobs, etc. Keep the focus on what is important and let God do the rest!

Isn't God Always There When We Need Him?

Come with me to a third grade classroom....

* There is a nine-year-old kid sitting at his desk and all of a sudden, there is a puddle between his feet and the front of his pants are wet.*

* He thinks his heart is going to stop because he cannot possibly imagine how this has happened. It's never happened be fore, and he knows that when the boys find out he will never hear the end of it. When the girls find out, they'll never speak to him again as long as he lives.*

* The boy believes his heart is going to stop; he puts his head down and prays this prayer, "Dear God, this is an emergency! I need help now! Five minutes from now I'm dead meat." *

 * He looks up from his prayer and here comes the teacher with a look in her eyes that says he has been discovered.*

 * As the teacher is walking toward him, a classmate named Susie is carrying a goldfish bowl that is filled with water. Susie trips in front of the teacher and inexplicably dumps the bowl of water in the boy's lap.*

 * The boy pretends to be angry, but all the while is saying to himself, "Thank you, Lord! Thank you, Lord!"*

 * Now all of a sudden, instead of being the object of ridicule, the boy is the object of sympathy. The teacher rushes him downstairs and gives him gym shorts to put on while his pants dry out. *

 * All the other children are on their hands and knees cleaning up around his desk.*

* The sympathy is wonderful. But as life would have it, the ridicule that should have been his has been transferred to someone else - Susie. She tries to help, but they tell her to get out. "You've done enough, you klutz!"*

* Finally, at the end of the day, as they are waiting for the bus, the boy walks over to Susie and whispers, "You did that on purpose, didn't you?" Susie whispers back, "I wet my pants once too."*

* May God help us see the opportunities that are always around us to do good.*

The little boy in this story could have potentially lost his friends and his self respect, until a caring heart came to his rescue. Have a caring heart today and assist someone before they lose something important to them.

Glimmers of Hope

Giving Glory to God

We serve an awesome God, who deserves praise, honor, and glory. So, let the praise begin.

A Holy Conversation

GOD: Angels, do you know what I was just thinking about?

ANGELS: What were you thinking about?

GOD: Christians seem to have forgotten what kind of power they have available and the devil keeps on deceiving them!

ANGELS: God, exactly what are you driving at?

GOD: I have made my children in such a way that when the people of the world are sitting, they would be standing, when the world is standing, they will stand out, when the world stands out, my children must be outstanding and when the devil dares the world to be outstanding, my people will be the standards to be used!

JESUS CHRIST: They (Christians) are also forgetting the words in Ephesians 1:3.

GOD: Please read it out!

ANGEL: PRAISE BE TO THE GOD AND FATHER OF OUR LORD JESUS CHRIST , WHO HAS BLESSED US IN THE HEAVENLY PLACES WITH EVERY SPIRITUAL BLESSING IN CHRIST .

ANGEL: So what do we do now since the end is almost near?

HOLY SPIRIT: My Presence is still among men and I will teach and remind the Christians of all that we have discussed. I will also make sure that they pass this message on!

JESUS CHRIST: I will also keep on interceding for them & stand in for them even in their weaknesses.

GOD: I will also make sure that I give to all those who ask of me, seek me and try to find me The blessings I have promised them through My Son, Jesus Christ will be delivered to all those who discover that I, Jehovah, am ready to bless them! Not because of any special things that they have done, but just because I LOVE THEM !

JESUS CHRIST: I will also give all My followers who are willing to pass this conversation on, enough strength to carry on!

ANGELS: We are all backing THE TRINITY and even the devil cannot stop us! How funny! Christians are finally taking over and ......

DEVIL (eavesdropping behind the gates): I hope you all heard! I will deploy more troops (demons) and make sure the Christians pray less, read their Bibles less, preach less and make sure <u>message</u> does not move anywhere!

The Greatest Man in History

Jesus had no servants, yet they called Him Master.

Had no degree, yet they called Him Teacher.

Had no medicines, yet they called Him Healer.

He had no army, yet kings feared Him.

He won no military battles, yet He conquered the world.

He committed no crime, yet they crucified Him.

He was buried in a tomb, yet He lives today.

I feel honored to serve such a Leader who loves us!

Jesus said ... "If you deny me before man, I will deny you before my Father in Heaven."

The Lord's Baseball Game

Freddy and the Lord stood by to observe a baseball game. The Lord's team was playing Satan's team. The Lord's team was at bat, the score was tied zero to zero, and it was the bottom of the 9th inning with two outs. They continued to watch as a batter stepped up to the plate named 'Love.' Love swung at the first pitch and hit a single, because "Love never fails."

The next batter was named Faith, who also got a single because Faith works with Love. The next batter up was named Godly Wisdom. Satan wound up and threw the first pitch. Godly Wisdom looked it over and let it pass: Ball one. Three more pitches and Godly Wisdom walked because he never swings at what Satan throws. The bases were now loaded. The Lord then turned to Freddy and told him He was now going to bring in His star player. Up to the plate stepped Grace. Freddy said, "He sure doesn't look like much!"

Satan's whole team relaxed when they saw Grace. Thinking he had won the game, Satan wound up and fired his first pitch. To the shock of everyone, Grace hit the ball harder than anyone had ever seen! But Satan was not worried; his center fielder let very few get by. He went up for the ball, but it went right through his glove, hit him on the head and sent him crashing on the ground. The roaring crowds went wild as the ball continued over the fence the Lord's team won!

The Lord then asked Freddy if he knew why Love, Faith and Godly Wisdom could get on base but couldn't win the game. Freddy answered that he didn't know why. The Lord explained, "If your love, faith and wisdom had won the game, you would think you had done it by yourself. Love, Faith and Wisdom will get you on base but only My Grace can get you Home.

'For by Grace are you saved, it is a gift of God; not of works, lest any man should boast." Ephesians 2:8-9

Psalm 84:11, "For the Lord God is a sun and shield; the Lord will give grace and glory; no good thing will He withhold from those who walk uprightly."

You Let the Devil Leave His Bags

YOU PUT THE DEVIL OUT, BUT DID YOU LET HIM LEAVE HIS BAGS?

You got out of a bad relationship because it was bad, but you are still resentful and angry (you let the devil leave his bags).

You got out of financial debt, but you still can't control the desire to spend on frivolous things (you let the devil leave his bags)

You got out of a bad habit or addiction, but you still long to try it just one more time (you let the devil leave his bags).

You said, I forgive you, but you can't seem to forget and have peace with that person (you let the devil leave his bags).

You told your unequally yoked mate that it was over, but you still continue to call (you let the devil leave his bags).

 You got out of that horribly oppressive job, but you are still trying to sabotage the company after you've left (you let the devil leave his bags).

 You cut off the affair with that married man/woman, but you still lust after him/her (you let the devil leave his bags).

You broke off your relationship with that hurtful, abusive person, but you are suspicious and distrusting of every new person you meet (you let the devil leave his bags).

You decided to let go of the past hurts from growing up in an unstable environment, yet you believe you are unworthy of love from others and you refuse to get attached to anyone (you let the devil leave his bags).

When you put the devil out, please make sure he takes his bags.

HAPPINESS KEEPS YOU SWEET

TRIALS KEEP YOU STRONG

AND SORROWS KEEP YOU HUMAN

SUCCESS KEEPS YOU GLOWING

BUT ONLY GOD KEEPS YOU GOING!

This year, Let the Devil Take His Bags With Him!

Be Blessed, Healthy and Happy

Keep God first in everything that you do!

Epilogue

When the storms of life come and we seem as though we are caught in an inescapable world wind of turmoil and despair, to keep our sanity, we must develop our faith. Faith development is part of our spiritual growth. Although there are areas that we excel in, each of us has weak areas within our individual lives as well. Therefore, we should allow the tests, trials, and obstacles to teach and develop us in the areas we fall short. To do this, we have to be open to who we are. None of us are perfect. If we are honest with ourselves, we will look for those areas so that we can know where the enemy is going to attack and where God wants to develop us.

So when the storms of life come, we will have roots that will go deep enough to sustain us as we stand firm in our faith walk. The devil will not be able to mow us down like last week's weeds. We will stand firm and be victorious as the royal priesthood that we are. So, take all the information that you read in the pages of this book and continue along your journey of spiritual development, but you must also have an active and strong prayer life. Therefore, we will end our journey of *Through the Storm* with a prayer.

Father God,

We come before you in the matchless name of Jesus banded one reader with another along with Cassundra White-Elliott, the author, in the spirit of unity. We thank you, Lord Father, for *Through the Storm* that you have provided for us to develop spiritually so that we may be able to stand against the wiles of the enemy and through the storms of life. Father, we now walk in the expectancy of victory and triumph that is provided by your hand. We thank you, Lord, for the opportunity to grow and develop in you as we draw closer to you. Father, we will take the information you gave us as knowledge and we will allow it to strengthen our roots. We declare that we will march forth and be indestructible. We will mount up with wings like an eagle; we will run and not grow weary; we will walk and not faint. We will keep our heads uplifted to the hills from whence cometh our help. We will hold fast to Isaiah 54:17 that says that, *"No weapon that is formed against thee shall prosper."* We will do all this while holding up the blood-stained banner while we proclaim Jesus Christ as Lord. We are your children and we walk in victory.

In the name of Jesus we pray,

Amen and Amen.

ABOUT THE AUTHOR

Dr. Cassundra White-Elliott resides in California with her family. As an English/Education professor, she teaches for various community colleges and universities.

When writing, she writes with the direction of the Holy Spirit, in an effort to share with God's people all that He has for them.

In addition to teaching and writing, Dr. White-Elliott also serves as an evangelistic teacher. She is also the founder of International Women's Commission, a ministry that serves the needs of the entire person, by attending to healing the mind, body, soul, and spirit.

Dr. White-Elliott holds a Ph.D. in Education, a Master's in English Composition, and a Bachelor's in Education. As education is her passion, in addition to sharing God's word, she desires to be instrumental in educating our nation's youth as she strives to eradicate the inequities of education that our minorities continuously suffer.

www.ingramcontent.com/pod-product-compliance
Lightning Source LLC
Chambersburg PA
CBHW072003090426
42740CB00011B/2060